THE UNIMPORTANCE
OF BEING OSCAR

by Oscar Levant

A SMATTERING OF IGNORANCE

MEMOIRS OF AN AMNESIAC

THE UNIMPORTANCE OF BEING OSCAR

OSCAR LEVANT

The Unimportance of Being Oscar

G. P. Putnam's Sons
New York

Library of Congress Catalog
Card Number: 68-20949

Acknowledgment is made to Richard G. Hubler for editorial assistance in the preparation of the manuscript.

PRINTED IN THE UNITED STATES OF AMERICA

To my daughters

Illustrations follow p. 98

Chapter 1

*M*Y wife, June, who has always helped me on books like this, is not my best friend, but she is my severest critic. To prove what I mean I must quote a remark attributed to the daughter of Mark Twain: "Father is writing and Mother is expurgating."

I certainly don't intend to identify myself with Mark Twain, but since I took up writing, my wife has declared that the greatest invention since the wheel is the eraser. Over the months that it takes me to write a book she constantly expurgates, heaves great sighs, and shrieks in anguish, "How many times must I listen to all this shit?"

After the publication of my last book, *The Memoirs of an Amnesiac,* I felt remorseful about a few of the slings and arrows that I directed at certain people.

Rosalind Russell, for instance. I kidded her for the sake of a quick laugh. It was a contemptible thing to do, and I want to apologize. First, because it was unkind—second, because there was a slight element of truth involved.

Actually, she is a wonderful woman, kind, warm, charitable; she possesses generous instincts; she is a good mother and a great success in life. (This is also a good description of Arlene Francis, in case I should ever need it.)

I hope Rosalind Russell will be compassionate enough to forgive me; compassion is the greatest human quality. (It's the quality I expect in everyone except myself.)

I am equally sorry that I quoted some of the things that Joe Kennedy said to me. I have no right to burden his children, or the career of Peter Lawford, with them.

I must also apologize for the withering remarks I made about Leonard Bernstein. But in my defense, I did *not* reveal how he used to play records of applause from his concerts. After all, I met Lenny eighteen years ago. I remember thinking then: Here is a young man who bears watching. Close watching.

As for Zsa Zsa Gabor—she's been a good sport about the things I've said about her. The fact that she pontificates on the two subjects at which she's failed—love and marriage—is beside the point.

Zsa Zsa's conversation is faster than her mind. I don't believe she could be analyzed—she doesn't seem to have a subconscious. Her face is inscrutable, but I can't vouch for the rest of her.

There is an impermanence about Zsa Zsa's marriages that I find appealing. Among her great accomplishments is the fact that she has been a good wife to at least five different husbands. At any rate, marriage is for bores. I mean Gabors.

(If Zsa Zsa is the lady I think she is, she will not accept my apology.)

* * *

There used to be an act in the old Club Eighteen in New York where a temporarily unemployed actor would step into a green spotlight in the middle of the floor and commence to recite Longfellow's poem which begins: "I shot an arrow into the air, It fell to earth, I knew not where." The reciter would pause, then sadly say: "I lose more damned arrows that way."

That has been my history of manufacturing jocose remarks. I lose more damn friends that way—such as S. N. Behrman, who inscribed his last play to me: With abiding love.

I also said to Christopher Isherwood, "You never invite me to your home."

He said, "I will, Oscar, I will."

That's what Whistler said to Oscar Wilde.

Whistler wrote *The Gentle Art of Making Enemies.* I must learn the "gentle" part.

I asked my publisher plaintively: "Why does June always emerge as the hero of my books?"

He said: "Endurance."

Six months ago Clifton Fadiman, the literary critic, asked me what would happen if June ever left me. I told him I wouldn't last twenty-four hours. But on mature reflection I cut that to three hours.

Part of her power over me lies in the fact that in our house she is the One in Charge of the Pills. They are now prescribed in meager amounts by my doctor, and doled out at night by my wife. What's more, I have given up reading everything I used to read when I was young. Now my wife reads everything.

I even developed a hostility toward the piano in the afternoon. People came to visit me and asked me to play for them. Suddenly I discovered that it was impossible for me to face the keyboard. June coaxed me, cajoled me, even threatened me—she claimed that I was getting even with the piano—but she finally came to believe that it was psychologically impossible for me to play after three P.M. Well, the piano knows where I am. I usually spend my days in my bedroom. One friend says I live the eremitic life of Proust—except for the fact that I do not have the cork-lined room which his sensibilities dictated. I sleep twenty hours a day, and during the other four hours I have the happy faculty for taking catnaps. My favorite day of the year is that one on which, in California, we go back to standard time—and lose an hour of the day.

I've become a homebody.

Sam Goldwyn, the movie producer, has always been very understanding. Once, after we had enjoyed a talk, he said: "I'd like to come to your house and see you some time."

"Fine," I said.

"When are you in?"

"I'm in for six weeks at a time," I said morosely.

Another friend, Jack Hansen, a tycoon who heads a string of JAX stores across the country, actually called me up one day and invited me to go out in the noonday sun and play softball. How do you like that? It could have been the start of a new TV Western show called *Sunstroke*.

Why, even the comb and brush on my bureau seem heavy when I lift them. For five years I never shaved myself, always going to a barber. That time is long gone; I now have the barber come to the house.

In producing three children, June has had three Caesareans. Our youngest was born in the summer when we lived in Westport, Connecticut. I remember Westport not only because of the children but also because of the twenty acres I bought there. They were almost totally unusable. They were so rough and overgrown that hardly a square yard was visible or even habitable. I think the previous owners must have been Lewis and Clark.

Around that early time I met John Steinbeck. I asked him

what to do if I ever came across any snakes on my property. "Just kick 'em in the belly," he said. Me?

I am increasingly impressed with Tolstoi these days. Not because of his genius but because he had the guts at the age of eighty to leave his wife. By that time the relationship between them must have been a good deal like the old couple in Robert Anderson's play, *You Know I Can't Hear You When the Water's Running.*

June was once asked if she loved me. "I don't know whether I love Oscar or not," she said evenly, "but if he wasn't around I'd probably miss him." This I call treacly sentimentality.

I also reminded my wife that Goethe said that a man was lucky if he had three perfect days in a whole life. My wife agreed with that. I asked her what her three perfect days were. She said at once: "The three days that I gave birth to the children." How would you react to that? She did not even give me one day.

One thing led to another, and finally I remarked to my wife that for over twenty-five years I had been surrounded by women —my wife and my three daughters. The only things that ever came up in conversation were hairdos, lipstick, and eyelashes. (Eyelashes mean nothing to me. I've never put my arms around an eyelash in a mad burst of passion.)

However, I have always been glad that my children were all daughters. I wouldn't have known how to control boys. I seem to lack the required authority. But with my daughters—well, I'm just one of the girls.

As a matter of fact, I am sometimes taken pretty much for granted by my family. But I suppose most husbands and fathers can say that.

In the middle of one busy schedule, my wife suddenly stopped short. "What day is it?" she asked absentmindedly.

"I don't know," I answered truthfully. "And I wouldn't tell you if I did," I added peevishly.

This attitude sometimes handicapped me in instructing my children. One night at the dinner table, I listened to my daughter describing some girlish feud. "You should never hold grudges," I said loftily.

There was a silence. June, changing the subject, said: "By the way, Oscar, so-and-so from New York phoned today and asked me to give you his regards."

My mood changed instantly. "Don't tell me that," I said irritably. "I haven't spoken to him for twenty years."

That reminds me of a suspicious thing about my own family. No one says Gesundheit to me anymore.

I yearn for affection from my family. I was overcome when one of my daughters spoke to me with emotion in her voice. I smiled lovingly at her. "Just for that, I may adopt you," I said.

When they are young, our children learn from us; when we are old, we learn from them. But unfortunately kids demand perfection from their parents. Our only chance is that maturity will help them to understand that we are imperfect. And we hope they will endure us anyhow.

One of my daughters used to bring home bits and pieces of student graffiti from UCLA for my amusement. She told me about a handbell standing alone on a desk. Beside it was a sign: IF NECESSARY, RING BELL. Below that, some anonymous psychology student had scribbled: THEN SALIVATE.

Another UCLA sign read: DO NOT WRITE ON THIS SIGN. Below it was scrawled: OKAY.

A third sign was evidently wholly student-inspired. It was a long arrow with the direction: OPHELIA! THIS WAY TO THE NUNNERY.

In a phone booth, a telephone number was inscribed with the message: ANY GIRL WHO WANTS A GOOD LAY CALL BOB.

BUT YOU'RE NEVER HOME! was written beside it.

Speaking of graffiti (the ancient art of anonymous inscription) Truman Capote has been quoted as saying that the most creative writing in America is on the wall of the men's room in New York's Fifty-third Street subway station.

And everyone has heard that the playwrights Albee and Newley got their titles *Who's Afraid of Virginia Woolf?* and *Stop the World I Want to Get Off* from graffiti signs.

My favorite is: THE MARQUIS DE SADE REALLY KNOWS HOW TO HURT A GUY.

My daughter also told me that at UCLA there is a NO SMOK-ING sign over the bust of Arnold Schoenberg. Some clown is always putting a cigarette in his mouth.

To me, that was sacrilegious.

When one of my daughters was of high school age, I discovered to my horror that she had read Simone de Beauvoir's book on the Marquis de Sade.

"What made you read about *him?*" I asked in astonishment.

"I'm interested in his political point of view," she replied calmly.

At UCLA she majored in political science. (And graduated with honors.) As did another daughter who I once overheard observe to a friend, "That's the most important handkerchief since Desdemona's!"

One of my daughters came home one afternoon when my old friend Adolph Green was visiting, and proudly told us that she got three *A*'s and a *B* in her courses.

"What was the *B* for?" inquired Adolph.

Why do people always seem to ask that?

When my wife decided to resume her acting career, it was with my blessing. In 1966 she appeared in two plays on the Los Angeles stage, one after the other. I got used to not seeing her for five hours every night. I told a friend, "I've grown unaccustomed to her face."

When June returned to the hearth after her last play closed, I said to my daughter, "Now, I miss not missing her."

I once made up one of my quarrels with my wife by a superb subterfuge. I was asked to do a TV show when she was mad at me, and I stipulated that she appear by my side. For that kind of notoriety, to say nothing of the propinquity, I knew she would forget her grudge.

Which leads me into my definition of a good husband—a man who is unattractive to other women. Or, if you prefer, a man whose wife is much too good for him.

T. S. Eliot is full of lines that are especially quotable. Such as "April is the cruellest month." I changed this to read "June." I have to find some way to keep people from calling her "Saint June."

But her temperament is a fact. One morning about three A.M., I woke her up to ask her for a forbidden pill. I did not really wake her up; I am sure she was only shamming, because I made a lot of noise. Do you know, she threw a glass of water and two slippers at me?

The next morning I managed to approach her. "You beat the hell out of me last night," I said.

Guess what she answered? "Show me the marks," she said.

I know where Nikita Khrushchev—when he was still head man in Russia—got his idea of putting dissident artists into a sanitarium and torturing them gently (Ward Seven). He got it from my wife.

It is true that no doctor in Beverly Hills or Los Angeles will even talk to me these days unless my wife okays it. Even their recording machines hang up on me. I said to one of them reproachfully, "After all, you know, my wife is not a cardiologist," but he did not answer. If I need a doctor now and then, I usually look in the Yellow Pages of the phone book—but even there, most of them know me. If they do come, they just give me one mild sedative and take themselves off. I never see them a second time. All this is based on the fact that they consider me, as one joker said, a "psychocondriac."

I was the trusting husband who taught June to play poker. She became one of the great poker players of Beverly Hills. But I gave poker up when I went into my deep depression. This leads up to the fact that one night she went out to a poker game and left me in a nervous state. I called up one of these new Los Angeles medical groups. Most of them have my name up on their bulletin board, I know, telling whoever takes my calls to pay no attention. But this was a new group, and I had great hopes. I called early and they agreed to visit me and I waited— for hours. Whenever I called back, they told me they were having an emergency. They had emergency after emergency. They never did come.

I could not figure out how they had got suspicious of me. I finally found the reason. I have an unlisted telephone number, but my daughters have another telephone with the number listed. The medical group called the girls, they referred them to the place where my wife was playing poker, and that canceled that.

On the other hand, it is true that sometimes I went so far as to call the police and fire departments to break down her door because she would not speak to me—but they never came.

They did come, though, on one occasion. One night I contracted pneumonia. I could hardly breathe, and the doctor, over the phone, told me wife to call the fire department's emergency squad. They brought an oxygen tank over and gave me some. Then my doctor's associate came in with a lone policeman. This infuriated me because the real doctor never sees me. I pointed weakly at the associate and croaked: "Arrest that man!"

Naturally, they paid no attention to me, and I was off to the hospital on a stretcher. But just before the ambulance left, my wife patted my hand, "I love you, too," she said. And as sick as I was I replied, "What do you mean, *too?*"

As I have said to my wife many times, a kind word is as good as a handful of pills. (But it does not last as long.)

I have made the statement that if I had the choice between the most beautiful girl in the world and three grams of Tuonol, I would take the latter. I stick by it.

At another time after I had complained about pains all over my body, I went into a hospital for a thorough checkup from chin to toes. The X-rays showed nothing amiss. My wife claims that when she told me the good news, my reply was: "Yes, but I've got a toothache."

I could write a good deal about dentists, too. One of my dentists was addicted to modern equipment. He was surrounded by chrome and flashing lights. The whole room in which he treated his patients was wired. Every time the phone rang, he was able to answer it with his head in my mouth.

Incidentally, he was a terrible dentist. He told me: "Don't eat anything hot or cold."

Plaintively, I asked: "What's left?"

Actually I have very few teeth left nowadays. But this dentist was terribly encouraging about it. "You have the same number of teeth as my mother did when she died," he reassured me.

When he worked on my teeth—which was often—he always hummed the same song, "I'll Get By as Long as I Have You." My wife goes to another dentist who takes care of many celebrities. While he fills her cavities, he also fills her in on all of Bob Hope's old jokes. (I should write a cookbook for people who have bad teeth.) (And while I'm at it, a cookbook for anorexia patients.)

My marriage, in my opinion, depends on the delivery of the

Sunday New York *Times*—especially the theatrical section and fashion ads.

Which reminds me. When I was married the first time, long, long ago, I bought my former wife Barbara a gift of clothes from the fashionable New York store Bergdorf-Goodman. That was on a Christmas—by New Year's our marriage had broken up.

In the months that followed, I was in no mood to pay the bill that kept coming back like a radish, so I ignored it. Finally they were going to take legal action. I sat down and wrote an amiable letter to the store suggesting a way to settle the matter: If they would forget about my debt, I in turn would bestow upon them the honor of a dedicee. My new composition for chamber orchestra would be entitled: *The Bergdorf-Goodman Sinfonietta.*

They were not interested in becoming a patron of the arts, so I paid the bill. But I still think it was a good idea.

Not too long ago, one of the girls in the Ziegfeld Follies, who broke a date with me and whom I never called again (I was like iron about things like that), sent me a letter (thirty-five years later), saying she was sorry. She had read my *Memoirs* and recognized herself in the book. She also enclosed her picture. It showed her with blonde hair, but I remembered her as a brunette.

"She must have dyed her hair," I said, showing the picture to June.

"That's gray hair," June said shortly.

My wife and I have had extended spells of not speaking to each other. I remember the winter of 1954 in New York. June was in California, and she and I did not speak for four months. I met an actress who tantalized me with the largest sleeping pill I have ever seen, but soon our affection curdled and she withdrew the pill. I said spitefully: "You look like the death mask of Beethoven." She liked that.

My compliments to women have not been uniformly successful. I once told a lovely model that she was a narcissist. She was very pleased. She thought I meant she had good taste.

Awed by the beauty of another fair one, I said to her: "You are my Opus One Hundred and Eleven." She slapped my face. I believe she thought I was trying to make her. Actually, I referred to the last and greatest sonata of Beethoven, a masterpiece. It was a unique compliment that got lost.

I have told Angie Dickinson, the eminently delectable actress, that she is starry-eyed about herself. But I like her outstanding social habit; she always kisses her friends, intimate or otherwise, full on the lips. One night she aimed at me and missed half my mouth.

"That's the first time you've missed," I told her.

So she kissed me three times.

I sighed. "Now you make me feel like a good Democrat again," I said. It was the only time I ever saw her lose her complacency. Angie is married to the talented composer-pianist-conductor Burt Bacharach. Musicians have always had an attraction for women. In my day the *New Yorker* once ran a two-line poem about me:

> Glamor girls pant
> For Oscar Levant.

I forget who wrote it, but what other rhymes could the poet use, considering the topic and subject?

I think the fashion of sandwiching a man between each woman at dinner parties is respectable and inspirational. But, as I told one of my hosts, never seat a dope addict next to a dope addict. They monopolize each other.

My wife has an enormous advantage. Whenever we enter a

room together, she automatically gets a wave of sympathy. One evening at a party, June left the room for a moment. When she came back she asked suspiciously what I was talking about.

"I have been quoting you all evening," I said meekly.

One young woman I have in mind occasionally exceeds the bounds of good taste, which talent endears her to me. She is the wife of a well-known Hollywood producer. We met at a party a couple of years ago. She was very amiable. June and I were sitting at a table with her while the others were dancing. At the end of the evening, she turned to June. "I love your husband," she stated. "Can I have him?"

June, her ramrod spine protruding all over the place, said stiffly: "Of course you can have him, but you must realize he has children who are older than you."

It was not quite accurate—not by a decade, anyway. But the odd thing about it was that June first gave me away and then made me out to be the Methuselah of our time. I remarked to a friend: "I'll never have an affair with *that* woman."

"Why not?" she asked with the calm that is indigenous to Southern California.

"Neither of us can drive," I explained.

What this means, naturally, is that I have lost my freedom. I do not mean by being married. I mean that in this day and age, if you give up driving a car, as I have, you lose your freedom. I simply cannot ask my wife to drive me to my mistress.

But I could not have gotten my driver's license renewed anyway. I would have had to give them a list of the mental hospitals that I have attended. That would have made the application heavier than the car itself.

A wealthy woman of my acquaintance, although growing older, is immediately responsive to anyone on whom her eye happens to light. One day a handsome boy of about twenty-one passed by, and her complexion turned florid with excitement.

She asked him to come and see her next day. Even her closest friend was shocked and chided her.

"Well," the amoretto replied, "all right. When we get old we'll have fourteen houses between us—and only each other. We'll visit the fourteen houses in wheelchairs."

I admire her. I always admire people who can break the bans of society without the slightest guilt feeling. In my case—I never cheat and I always get caught. The main reason I can never fall in love again is that I cannot bear to tell the story of my life all over again.

I've trained myself to do without love, and I must say I've been afforded great opportunities.

In reality, in regard to sex, I personally find it very difficult to stand involvement of any kind. I met a girl who offered to have an affair with me. "If I made love to you," I told her, "I would have to bring an oxygen tent."

When I last saw the actor Barry Sullivan, who is constantly changing wives, I said to him, "Why don't you marry me and get it over with?"

I see by the papers, too, that the old gag originated by Oliver Wendell Holmes, "Oh, to be sixty again!" is making the rounds once more. I think this is significant.

Pretty soon I will be an interesting study in geriatrics—growing old disgracefully. For the last few years women tell me that their fathers knew me. It is a great pity that men should become so intimidated by age. I believe that Congress should pass a law decreeing that Ursula Andress should make herself immediately available to all elderly, sex-hungry men.

It was sex that lost the Prince of Wales the throne of England. In my opinion, it is sex that fucks up every marriage.

A lot of my contemporaries—people that I have loved or been very close to—have died recently. The reactions of their widows have been quite revealing. The deaths of their husbands have resulted in great, though well-concealed, relief.

Maybe this outlook is all summed up in a remark that a woman patient once made to me in a mental hospital that we shared. She had been married four times, and she said: "There are worse things than being alone."

I have my likes and dislikes in this world, and they are based on my own standards. One of them demands that I like the actress Carroll Baker. I like her because she comes from Pennsylvania, near Scranton. That means she is anthracite. John O'Hara, the author, from Pottsville, Pennsylvania, is also anthracite. Since I come from Pittsburgh, I am bituminous. We people of the coal world must stand together.

When I was a child my mother used to tell me, "You'll never be a Paderewski, but you'll never be lonely." I guess she meant I would always have the piano baring its eighty-eight ivory teeth at me. Actually, I always liked music and piano-playing. Nobody had to force me to play—the great dance-band pianist Eddy Duchin told me that his mother used to whip him to make him practice. Why force them, if they don't want to do it?

The story of my life has consisted of putting too much faith in institutions. When I was a young man my mother used to tell me to send my money home to her. She told me she would put it in the bank for me. I did it to show my faith. She put her money in with mine to show her faith. The bank failed for both of us.

As was the custom of her generation, my mother, a music lover, had a collection of plaster busts of composers. When she learned that Wagner was Hitler's favorite composer, she couldn't bring herself to throw out his statue. Instead, she displayed her anger by turning the Wagner bust around to face the wall.

She was a very knowledgeable woman in rather recondite fields. Once on *Information Please* I was asked the name of Lenin's wife. I had no idea. My mother, listening to the show at home, shrieked the answer. Unfortunately, I could not hear her.

The measure of your success is when you call up your mother and ask her: "How was it?" I remember when I called my mother up to ask her that, after a very successful concert. She said: "Again, the *Rhapsody in Blue.*" But then she always said that.

When he was a young man S. N. Behrman scored a hit with his first play, *The Second Man.* It had Alfred Lunt in the leading role and was a play of quality as well as a commercial success.

His mother saw the play.

"Sam," she asked, "why don't you get married?"

Mrs. Rose Gershwin, mother of George and Ira, attended the opening night of Moss Hart's smash hit, *Lady in the Dark,* the sophisticated musical about psychoanalysis.

At intermission Moss was jubilant. "What do you think of it?" he asked Mrs. Gershwin.

"Sveet," was her comment.

On the other hand, at the opening of the Gershwin show *Oh, Kay!* Papa Gershwin's reply to "How do you like it?" was: "I gotta like it!"

Norman Granz, the personal manager of Ella Fitzgerald and a former jazz concert promoter, built a small record company, Verve, into a highly successful enterprise. He eventually sold out to the MGM record company for a couple of million. With great pride he showed the enormous check to his mother. "I always knew you were lucky," she announced.

The mother of a young pianist once asked my advice: Was there a shortcut to eliminate the drudgery of practice? "I've been looking for a shortcut for twenty years," I told her. "Now I'm practicing."

Another woman asked if her boy could become a prodigy. "Sure," I said. "Just lie about his age."

Speaking of Norman Granz, we once had a luncheon date at a restaurant at one o'clock. My reaction to the place was so violent that I could not stand to eat there. We went to another; that looked worse. We tried a third, and then a fourth. By the time it was four-thirty, we had canvassed seven restaurants. I had found fault with all of them. So Granz took me home. "Say, Norman," I said as he let me out of the car, "how about dinner?"

My opinion is that my relationships with women are related to the fact that I was rarely kissed when I was a child. There were three boys before I came into the family. My mother told me that she had always wanted a daughter. I told her that I would try to do my best but, as far as I know, it did not work out. My father, I remember, kissed me once. I was not his favorite child, but I cannot blame him.

As a kid, I never liked being alone. We lived behind the store, and my parents would usually go out for a walk at night. They would lock me in—for safety, they said. Once, trying to get out—I must have been seven or eight years old—I punched a hole through a glass door with my right hand. A week later, I did the same thing with my left hand. The glass practically cut one of my fingers off. For an embryonic pianist that would have been quite a handicap.

I recall some of the youngsters in my old neighborhood who studied law and medicine. But after thirty-five years of psychoanalysis I can safely say that I was the only one who studied to be a patient.

I told one of my legion of doctors that when my mother died, on my way to the cemetery the first movement of the Brahms Violin Concerto came into my head. I could not get rid of the main theme.

This work of Brahms, of course, was one of the favorite pieces of Jascha Heifetz, the celebrated violinist. It is easy for me to remember how much of an impact Heifetz had on the American

Jewish world when he first came over here as a *Wunderkind* in 1917. He was the one that all Jewish families kept pointing out to their musically inclined children. He was the great example of what could be done if the unfortunate kid merely kept playing his scale exercises. I was no exception.

So this was one of my unrealistic torments. I always felt that somehow I did not fulfill the dream of my mother. Actually I was a success as a pianist and my mother was very happy, but my subconscious was dissatisfied. It has been that way ever since.

I have been analyzed so many times by so many psychoanalysts that I refuse to be analyzed any more. When I do go, it is usually just to make expensive conversation. As far back as 1953 an analyst urged me to stop. "You're addicted to analysis," he said.

The effort of all psychoanalysis, they tell me, is to break the pattern of a personality. All they ever do is to shift the individual from one pattern to another. No pattern, once established, is ever broken.

I think one of the secrets of treatment is to recognize that progress is so painfully slow. If you can adjust yourself to that tempo, then you might make progress. A prominent movie actress reintroduced herself to me about six months after she had a personal tragedy. She said, "What shall I do?"

I said, "Just realize that emergence is gradual."

People always think that some mysterious miracle will transform them. I do not say that it is false; I merely say that I have never seen it happen.

I realize that there are new psychiatric terms every year. The jargon changes with the times. Not only has dementia praecox gone, but its substitute, schizophrenia, is on its way out. "Id" is now an old-fashioned term. Nevertheless, the more they change, the more they stay the same, in someone else's words.

Analysis these days is reduced to two words: adapt and cope. I find it hard to do either.

I discovered that the skill of the psychiatrists is not always as wondrous as it is supposed to be. It is only on television that you see complete revelations and cures in psychiatry. Actually, after the thrill of discovering a man who shows complete interest in you and after the pleasure of talking to him about yourself wears off, you lapse into your old pattern anyway. It does do some good in the beginning, but then comes the odious period when there is nothing left to say. You start repeating yourself.

Nor does the analyzing of dreams help much. Dream interpretations vary so greatly with each doctor that I do not know how they arrive at any sensible conclusion. My first analyst in New York (who only charged me five bucks a visit) was by far the best on dreams. I am convinced that they all guess, that it's complete guesswork.

But, at any rate, one of my early analysts got screen credit for producing the dreams in that picture called *Spellbound,* with Ingrid Bergman.

One night I walked into a restaurant and greeted a man: "Hello, how are you? How's your wife? How are your children? How's your partner? How's your brother? How's your sister?" Then I explained that my analyst told me I'm not solicitous enough about people.

My private name for another psychiatrist was Old Unfaithful. I remember discussing Shakespeare with him. "There's a lot of Freud in Shakespeare," he informed me.

"It's the other way around," I informed him.

It is like the time that my analyst told me I was afraid of death. "I know," I said. "I've learned to live with it."

"But," said the analyst, "along with that fear is a death wish."

The last time I went to see him I complained: "I said something that upset me."

He looked at me as though I were crazy.

"*You* said something that upset you?" he asked incredulously.

A writer I know was very thin when he started his analysis. He suddenly got very fat. Somebody said he swallowed his analyst.

Dr. Emmanuel Libman, the late great diagnostician, declared that lay analysts were Freud's revenge on the medical profession.

And a psychiatrist in attendance at Mt. Sinai Hospital in Los Angeles said that a psychologist was to psychiatry what a chiropodist is to a surgeon.

He destroyed my faith in everything I don't believe in.

When I went into one mental hospital I never had any dreams, but I always tried to, just to make my psychiatrist happy. One of the unusual things that happened when I was incarcerated—a mild term for it—was that a doctor came to me and asked if there was anything he could do for me. It was the only time I recall any doctor asking me such a kindly thing. I thought of Richard Wagner and the Ring operas. In *Die Walküre*, Brünnhilde is put to sleep by Wotan for seventeen years or so until she is awakened by a pure young man who is, of course, Siegfried. I replied: "Put me to sleep like Wotan."

I got so that I hated the hospital. After a certain period I was permitted to go home for a few hours a day. By that time my home also seemed strange to me. My friend Goddard Lieberson came to visit me while I was "on leave."

"My home is a nice place to visit," I told him, "but I'd sure hate to live here."

When I phoned my doctor, a secretary asked, "Who's calling?"

"Dr. Fidel Castro," I replied as I gave her my number. The secretary automatically answered: "Thank you, Doctor. He'll call you back."

In the New York *Times* I read an article by the music critic

Harold Schonberg about the closing of the Metropolitan Opera House. It reminded me of some stories that I wanted to tell him. I picked up the phone. "Please get me the New York *Times*," I said to the operator.

"What city is that in?" she asked.

When I was discharged from the hospital, I lamented to my doctor: "This, I suppose, means that I am going to be my old self again—God forbid!"

Somebody once stared at me and said that I reminded him of the French movie star Jean-Paul Belmondo.

"I'm his stunt man," I told him.

I dislike people who do not believe that I am really sick. Two weeks ago a friend of mine called me up. "What's the bad word?" was his opening crack.

My old friend, Sam Behrman, has been quoted as saying: "There's nothing wrong with Oscar that a really first-class miracle couldn't cure." Possibly true. All I know is that when the magazine *Town and Country* ran an article on "How to Become a Neurotic," it offered a weekend with me as first prize. Still, I have often seriously thought of giving a course at the local university. I would call it: Self-Destruction 103. I am interested in sensory perception. Even plain perception is good enough. Extrasensory perception becomes a matter between you and the drugstore.

Some people have commented, right in my presence, that they do not think I am all there. I do not believe the word "there" is correct in this case. What they mean to say is that they do not believe I am all *here*.

In a discussion about what to entitle a book after one has written one's memoirs, Eric Ambler says it is invariably *The Latter Years*. In my case it should be: *So Little Time and So Little to Do*. However, I had just about decided to call this book *The Last Twenty-four Hours in the Life of Jim Bishop* when I remembered a letter I received after my *Memoirs* were published.

"You chose the wrong title for your book," said the unknown letter writer. "You should have named it: *Odd Man, Inside Out.*"

Chapter 2

I CANNOT claim to know too much about songwriting these days. I have been away from it too long. Still I do know from experience that songwriters are a curious group of people, to say the least. Perhaps it comes from unfulfilled creative credit. No one knows exactly where a song comes from. Sometimes it comes from an idea or a title or lyrics or the tune —or it may be a wisecrack, an offhand remark, or a disguised steal. Once it is put together, it is tangible, and the mystery is dissipated. Credit is a problem: the tune writer usually gets first billing, but it was not that way, for instance, with the team of Gilbert and Sullivan. The feud between those two is not unusual. There is not always complete rapport between the one who writes the words and the one who writes the notes. Usually the musician has the easier time of it.

Alan Jay Lerner, one of the few lyricists who gets first billing, is a deadline writer. He sweats blood to the very end. When he was working on a show with composer Richard Rodgers, he had fought his way through to the end of one set of lyrics. With a feeling of relief and the prospect of two weeks off, he sent them to his partner by messenger. He claims he had just taken a shower and a shave when Rodgers rang him up. The call was to tell him that the music was ready. Their working habits clashed, everything went wrong, and they finally called the whole thing off.

I happened to be in New York the day after Alan Lerner's musical *On a Clear Day You Can See Forever* opened. It got mixed critical notices. I knew he would be licking his wounds, so I called him up to offer some comfort. One of the girls I talked to in his office told me: "Mr. Levant, you're a very kind man."

It touched me. "If I am, it's a well-kept secret," I said.

To me, Alan Lerner is the most lyrical of lyric writers. My friendship with him goes back to the old radio days when he was the head writer for the *Hildegarde Show* and I was a frequent guest. We were also associated with the Academy Award musical picture *An American in Paris*. Alan won an Oscar for his original screenplay for that picture.

Movie producer Arthur Freed had signed Alan to an exclusive contract after Alan had written two stage musicals—one with Frederick Loewe and the other with Kurt Weill. Neither had been big hits, but they had shown promise and originality.

Freed had great faith in Alan's ability and felt that he was the most talented young lyricist and librettist since Oscar Hammerstein II. Lerner and Loewe did the score for Freed's successful picture *Gigi*, and Alan wrote the screenplay—based on the

French movie adapted for the screen by the great Colette from her own short story.

Not so fortunate was the film version of the Lerner-Loewe musical *Brigadoon*. The play had been bought by MGM at the instigation of Gene Kelly—a mistake as it turned out; the leading role was written originally for a singer, not a dancer. Considering the fact that it had been a hit on the stage and the winner of the critics' award, Alan thought it inexcusable that the picture had not fared as well. He noted with exasperation, "It could be a hit in a phone booth!" I remembered his remark when *Brigadoon* won the 1967 Emmy Award as the best television musical show.

Alan, who came from an affluent family (Lerner Stores), is urbane, well-educated, an incurable romantic, and a nail biter. He knows a good song when he writes one, and his talent for casting his own plays is perfection. For example: Rex Harrison and Julie Andrews in *My Fair Lady;* Richard Burton and Robert Goulet in *Camelot*.

As a young man his hero was Larry Hart, the lyric writer, and he now rates T. S. Eliot as the poet of the century. He adored his father and asked him for his approval when his first wife insisted on a Catholic ceremony.

"It would be all right with me," said his father kindly, "if you were married by a lama."

Alan also remembered a paternal observation: "You'll never really be married until you marry a Frenchwoman." Alan met his fourth wife, Micheline, an attractive French lawyer, when she called him about tickets for *My Fair Lady*. I thought this a great start for any marriage, but now Alan is once again happily married—for the fifth time.

At the peak of his enormous success and during a temporary phase of notoriety, Alan went to live at the Waldorf Towers— the same hotel where his father had lived many years before.

On his arrival, he was greeted by an old-time employee of the hostelry who remembered him as a boy.

"What have you been doing all these years?" asked the em-
Such is fame.
ployee politely.

Alan was a classmate of President Kennedy at Choate and Harvard. And he never knew that his song "Camelot" had been a Presidential favorite. It was not until after the tragedy, when Mrs. Kennedy revealed the story publicly, that Alan learned of it. He wondered why the President never mentioned it to him on any of the occasions that he had seen him. It can only be assumed that President Kennedy's well-known abhorrence for any show of sentimentality had prevented him from doing so.

My Fair Lady is without question the biggest musical smash of all time, with its incomparable score and its witty, wry Shavian book. Alan researched the play *Pygmalion* with profound dedication to G. B. Shaw. Secretly, however, he wasn't completely happy with the movie version.

The rivalry between competitors on the stage is everlasting. When Marc Blitzstein made an opera called *Regina* out of Lillian Hellman's *The Little Foxes,* I was with the party that stayed up late to catch the first reviews. Some artists have the human but unpleasant habit of reading them out loud as they come in. When they are good, the result is intoxicating. In this case, they were not good.

With the group was a friendly rival, a composer, who shall be nameless, as they say. As the reviews got worse and worse, the composer—who was pretty much unknown at the moment— grew more and more ecstatic. It was remarkable to see how someone else's failure enlivened his evening. Another man, a playwright, is the only other person I know who is the same about his competitors. He glows radiantly as the bad news pours in. It all reminds me of La Rochefoucauld's canny observation:

"There is something in the misfortune of even our dearest friends that is not entirely displeasing to us."

Noel Coward attended the opening night of the Max Gordon-produced musical called *The Cat and the Fiddle*. At intermission, smiling radiantly, he put his arms around the producer and said with great affection: "Max, darling, it stinks!"

When Noel was touring the English provinces with one of his new shows, the producer of the vehicle said to him bluntly, "What the show needs is more laughs."

Noel impaled him with a look.

"For instance?" he asked icily.

Getting laughs always sounds so easy. Adolph Green, of the writing team of Comden and Green, told me of a request from one of *his* producers. "In this scene," announced the producer blithely, "we'll need ten minutes of airy persiflage!" Which reminds me that I once observed about Michael Kidd, the New York dance director, that he made modesty a vice.

Musicals are always difficult to produce. The synchronization of music, scenery, action, and continuity is the hardest job in the theater. The ensemble is the thing, even to such details as height: Rosalind Russell has to be surrounded by tall people, Gene Kelly by short ones.

The whole process comes down to selection. But not always the wisest heads are immune from sentiment. I remember that Vincent Youmans, the greatly talented composer who died much too young, always wanted a success specifically in the Belasco Theatre, a prestige theater in New York. It was Max Dreyfus, one of the smartest men in the song business, who finally yielded to his whim. He backed one of his shows there for him, *Hit the Deck*. There were three top hit songs, including "Hallelujah!" It played for weeks to SRO. But the place was so small that it lost thousands of dollars a week.

Another show of that era was *Oh, Kay!* with a score by George and Ira Gershwin, and a young English star, Gertrude Lawrence. The memorable song from that hit was "Someone to Watch over Me."

In 1958, when I had my Los Angeles television show, I received the first of a series of letters from the late Laurence Stallings. We had not met, but I was familiar with his reputation as a literary critic, coauthor of the play *What Price Glory?* and scenario writer of the legendary silent movie *The Big Parade*. His memories of *Oh, Kay!* bear repeating:

> Your stuff about George Gershwin was unbeatable two weeks ago; but were you old enough to catch those rehearsals of "Oh, Kay" at the Music Box? Heywood Broun was drama critic of the World, and I was his drama editor. I could get all my work done with contacts during those rehearsals. Everyone got there in the morning, male and female, as soon as they could pull on their britches. George had two long Steinways in the pit, with Phil Ohman and Vic Arden at the keys—there was no Mason & Hamlin Upright on the stage with the guy in the undershirt beating the tempo. The business began around ten in the morning, and went on until well past dinner time. George would run up and down the aisles listening to his score, and then dash down and leap into the pit to say: "No, no . . . try it this way" and then he himself would play an hour or so. Chorus girls never stood around the wings: they were all busy copying and understudying Gertrude Lawrence, who was at her immortal loveliest and best. . . . Some folks came with box lunches, and others brought along the houseboy to rush the coffee and sandwiches. . . . I don't see how Harold Ross ever got the New Yorker published those four weeks; for the entire staff, led by Peter Arno, arrived with the opening chords. . . . It was a remarkable first night; everyone in the audience knew every note of the score; and a lot of folks could have jumped into the pit and played right along with Vic and Phil.

> Play some of that score sometimes!

Ira Gershwin, the brother of George (I only identify him because unbelievably he was once referred to as "George's lovely wife, Ira"), is always a stickler for facts. He wants the truth, the whole truth, and nothing but the truth—in anything with which he is connected, anyway.

One of his hobbies is writing indignant letters to correct history. He wrote one to Max Gordon, the producer. Max had published a book which failed to mention two flop plays in which Ira participated. I thought Ira should be grateful to Max for omitting all mention, but, no, Ira was irate. He wrote him instantly, demanding the correction. When Oscar Hammerstein wrote a gentle preface to a Kern-Hammerstein song book, he inadvertently declared that it was the first of its kind, without a qualifying adjective. Ira wrote another factual letter to his old friend. He pointed out the indubitable fact that the first book of the sort was written many years before by Harry B. Smith, the lyricist and librettist for Victor Herbert. Who else would have known?

Ira Gershwin is more of a listener than a talker, but his quiet sense of humor has long earned him the title, bestowed upon him by friends, of Pixie.

There was a gloomy interlude way back in 1927 when *Strike Up the Band,* words and music by George and Ira Gershwin, book by George Kaufman and Morrie Ryskind, flopped dismally at its tryout in Philadelphia.

One evening during the disastrous run, George, Ira, and Kaufman were standing outside the Shubert Theater, after the overture had started, brooding over the knowledge that the audience inside barely filled three rows of seats.

As they stood there disconsolately, a taxi pulled up to the curb and out stepped two men elegantly attired in spats, bowler hats, and moustaches. What's more, they actually went to the box office and bought tickets.

The trio outside the theater watched wordlessly as the Victorian-looking gentlemen disappeared into the theater.

A second passed. Ira cleared his throat.

"Gilbert and Sullivan have arrived to fix up the show," he announced.

Ira's remark threw the two Georges into hysterical laughter, providing a much needed hiatus from the unrelieved gloom.

On his leisure side, Ira likes to indulge in obsessions. One is that he can play at the racetrack with the name G-E-R-S-H-W-I-N. He tries to pick eight horses in succession, the initials of whose names will spell that magic word. This is a fairly unlikely bet, but he still likes to indulge himself.

Another obsession of Ira's is an eternal desire to fill an inside straight. So far the shuffle has not blessed him, but it was the desire of his life during one floating Hollywood poker game. This was a rather famous thing which was finally broken up by the police, almost on fiat of the Los Angeles City Council. It was composed of John Garfield, Charlie Coburn, Morrie Ryskind, Ira, and anyone else they could find. Garfield usually brought a copy of the Communist *Daily Worker* under his arm to unnerve Ryskind. Morrie was then—as now—a conservative's conservative. Inevitably the conversation always turned to the "common man." His virtues were loudly explained in between demands to "shuffle the cards!" At last Ryskind, in exasperation, demanded of Garfield: "Just who is this common man?" Without speaking, Garfield pointed at Ira.

Ira once got mad because I referred to him as "eccentric."

"I'm not eccentric," he protested. "I'm the most normal man in the world!"

"I know," I said. "That's what makes you eccentric."

That made Ira mad all over again.

I remember when he was given the manuscript of a novel written by a woman friend who had hopes of having it published. To his astonishment it turned out to be the dirtiest, most pornographic book he had ever read. When the lady mentioned that she intended to use a *nom de plume,* Ira suggested she call herself Henrietta Miller.

I think it was the *Saturday Review* that at one time asked all the songwriters it could find for their favorite song. The balloting ended decisively, as they say, with Jerome Kern's "All the Things You Are," an excellent choice.

The matrix of American show music goes back only as far as Jerome Kern. (Victor Herbert was born in Ireland.) But Kern became, as time went on, more and more "flowery" in his melodies. This is not unusual. People tend to get more sentimental as they grow older, and it comes out most obviously in music. Songwriters usually start out very simply, then gradually grow more intricate—and words come harder than tunes. Cole Porter told Ira Gershwin, "As I get older, the tunes are easy to write but I find it impossible to write lyrics"—and he never would let anyone else do it for him.

I knew Cole Porter, but I never was close to him. He had a small, very tight periphery of defense. Very few could penetrate it. I was very fond of all his music. I suggest, as a matter of fact, that the State Department add a question to applications for passports. It should read: Do you love the songs of Cole Porter? Anyone who does not answer in the affirmative under oath should not be permitted to travel abroad; he is a pseudo-American citizen.

I have known Jerry Kern's daughter Betty since she was seven years old. The last time I saw her I said, "Your father was the best."

Her face lighted up. "Do you really mean that?" she asked.

"Not only the best," I said, "but the first."

It is true—he was the first; but if Cole Porter had had a child, I'd have said the same to him.

In 1953, when Cole Porter's *Can-Can* was produced in New York, the critics rapped it, especially the score. After the opening, I met Dick Rodgers. I said how dreadful it was that it had been so unmercifully criticized.

"Well, it all evens itself out," Dick said. I knew he was referring professionally to the ecstatic notices that Porter's show *Kiss Me, Kate* had received in 1948, five years earlier.

One of my own favorite tunes, "Manhattan," by Rodgers and Hart, is a lovely thing but a misfit. It is written about a city, but its music is very pastoral.

In the twenties I used to go to parties at the house of Larry Hart. I happened to meet Teddy Hart, the actor, at a recent opening. He saw me and piped up in his high, crackling voice: "I used to see you at my brother's!" Evidently he thought I had been hiding in a cave for forty years.

Another songwriter, Harold Arlen, is held in the highest esteem by his colleagues. His impressive list of songs includes "Stormy Weather," "Let's Fall in Love," "Ac-cent-tchu-ate the Positive," "That Old Black Magic," "Come On, Get Happy," "One for the Road," "The Man That Got Away"—and, with Yip Harburg, the score for *The Wizard of Oz.*

The compelling manner in which Harold sings his own songs is highly personalized—he turns himself on and enjoys his own performance as much as his listeners do. His voice has the timbre of an Hebraic chant combined with the undulating quaver of a blues singer. It could be said that his singing style evolved from his early environment; his father was a cantor, and Harold got his start writing songs for the old Cotton Club shows in Harlem.

An item involving his singing took place during the run of *House of Flowers,* for which he wrote the music and Truman Capote wrote the words and book. The show was not too successful, but there was an album made. At the recording session everything went well and the cast was dismissed. When the tape was played back for the technicians, it was discovered that one high note sung by Diahann Carroll had not been true. No problem—Harold was present. He sat in and sang the note, and no one knew the difference.

I recall in the thirties, when the Coney Island boardwalk

and Forty-second Street in Manhattan were on their way to becoming blood cousins, I came across a "character analyst" with his little stand. With me were Irving Berlin and Curly Harris, a public relations man. They decided to have the "analyst" read their palms. He said to Curly: "You have great artistic talent." To Irving, he said: "You are a good businessman."

I hardly think it is possible for any expert to get more confused than that.

Irving once had an incident which intrigued me. When his oldest daughter was about thirteen, she had a luncheon date with a boy. For some reason the date was called off. Irving, in an attempt to cheer her up, said: "I want you to feel free to talk to me. I don't care what it is, I'll understand."

"You really mean that?" she asked.

He assured her that he did.

"All right," she said softly. "I just think that I prefer the score of *Top Hat* to that of *White Christmas*."

Since they are both Berlin movie scores, I could not see how this could upset anyone, but Mrs. Berlin was displeased. Her opinion is that Irving's songs are also his children and they should be liked equally.

In its early years, as everyone knows, the *New Yorker* nearly went out of business. It was rescued by an excellent and provocative article by Mrs. Berlin (Ellin Mackay). She is the wonderful woman who said: "The most frightening beginning of a sentence is when someone says to me: 'May I be frank?'" I agree: That is a four-word intimidation.

And the Berlin daughter, mentioned in the story above, is now Mary Ellin Barrett, the author of a highly acclaimed first novel.

Recently, I was berating my loss of some items in my memory and said to Irving in a typical exaggeration: "I can't recall the last ten years."

"Who wants to recall them?" asked Irving gloomily.

After twenty years, *Annie Get Your Gun* with its wonderful Berlin score was successfully revived last year, on stage as well as on television. Ethel Merman again played her original role. The span of her career has been remarkable.

Ethel was always the most unassuming of stars. She seemed as if she were always glad to get a job. After her first show, she had a date the next day with George Gershwin at his apartment on Riverside Drive in New York. She arrived. He held up the newspapers. "Read these," he said. "You're a star." Her amazement was genuine; she was completely unaware that there were such things as reviews.

In her prime, all the great songwriters wanted to write for Ethel. With her loud clear voice and rocketlike projection, she could put over a song as well as a show. As Irving Berlin said, "You'd better not write a bad song for Ethel because you'll *hear* it!"

In a discussion about her directors, Ethel gave credit to Jerome Robbins for being the most helpful in *Gypsy*, and she said about Joshua Logan, who directed *Annie*, "He did one important thing—he gave me that goofy awestruck expression I used when I was mooning over Frank Butler."

According to a friend who attended a church service with Ethel, she also belts out the hymns in her well-known raucous-like manner. The effect must be startling, albeit refreshing.

The only other stage star in the same league as Merman is Mary Martin. Over the years she has had many hit shows to her credit, with *South Pacific* and *The Sound of Music* her greatest triumphs. Also, of course, *Peter Pan*. That was filmed as a television special and is now run every year as a sort of traditional Christmas treat.

Mary made such a great impact in her first show on Broadway that on opening night I remember thinking: What a night for jealousy!

The song that she sang was Cole Porter's "My Heart Belongs to Daddy"—take away the words, and it is one of the most Yiddish tunes ever written. Just hum it and see. (If you are old enough to remember it.) I don't know how to explain it—Cole Porter's genetic background was completely alien to any Jewishness.

As for Mary, she is a lady of inviolate character—exemplary, disciplined, and dedicated. I recall with pleasure her lyrical voice, her engaging charm, the many roles she has created. I also say, with affection, that Mary Martin is the Twiggy of musical comedy.

One of the great entertainers of the century, certainly its oldest living star, is Maurice Chevalier. He has sustained his ability to perform as a one-man attraction. Al Jolson was in this category; Judy Garland is another. Of the new generation, only Barbra Streisand belongs.

Introduced to New York audiences by Florenz Ziegfeld at the New Amsterdam Roof Garden in the twenties, Chevalier went to Hollywood in the early musical days, brought there by Jesse Lasky of Paramount Studios. With his roguish charm, good looks, and individual singing style, he was an immediate sensation. His pictures were sophisticated continental farces, directed mostly by Ernst Lubitsch. Rodgers and Hart wrote a marvelous score for one of them with such songs as "Mimi," "Lover," and "Isn't It Romantic." The song "Louise" by Dick Whiting (Margaret Whiting's father) and Leo Robin, became Chevalier's trademark. His last picture in that era was *The Merry Widow* with Jeanette MacDonald. He returned to France during the war years, returning in the forties to appear once more on stage with his one-man show.

When he resumed his movie career, he was an elderly character actor, yet his youthful spirit and zestful bounce remained. Alan Lerner had written a part for him in *American in Paris*, but for reasons unknown another French actor, Georges Guetary, played the role. Chevalier did play in *Gigi*, however, and received Alan's highest term of approbation, "a real pro."

Over the years I have had but fleeting encounters with Chevalier. On one occasion we discussed the old days. His negative reaction to two people surprised me. When we talked of Lubitsch, I got the impression that his early director had been too overpowering for him. His only meeting with G. B. Shaw did not seem to impress him either. This I understand— not from my point of view certainly, but from the point of view of a Frenchman.

Shaw's plays have had very little success in France. There could be two reasons for this: One, his plays have been adapted in France by a mediocre writer, personally appointed by Shaw. Two, and more important, there is no love or sex in a Shaw play. How could that possibly appeal to the French temperament?

Chevalier as a young man had been a protégé of the French star Mistinguett, and he had been married once, and divorced, when he was very young.

He confessed, on a television show, that the image of Al Jolson as this country's greatest entertainer and single attraction had intimidated him when he first arrived in this country. And he proudly displayed an old photo that Al had inscribed to him.

Two years ago Chevalier wrote me about my *Memoirs* with a flattering request that I inscribe his copy. I was, of course, delighted by his interest. He wrote in his letter, "Wishing you to be able to go on laughing at your miseries for a long, long time."

My wife liked that.

Al Jolson came by his trademarked remark, "You ain't heard nuthin' yet," by way of desperation. He said he was once on a program where his act followed that of Enrico Caruso—and that only by shouting his egoistic inspiration was he able to hold the crowd.

Jolson and Eddie Cantor always had a red-hot rivalry going in show business. Eddie told me of an incident that occurred when they were both appearing in Chicago as stars of their own shows. During the run, Eddie became so sick that he could barely make it to the stage—but he was determined not to close his show and leave the field to Jolson. His appearances went on and on, until he finally became so weak that he had no choice but to cancel. Much to Cantor's surprise, Jolson immediately closed *his* show. It was then that Cantor learned that Jolson was also very sick. Unaware of Cantor's illness, Al had suffered through the same ordeal in order not to give the advantage to Eddie. Ever after that, Jolson said gratefully: "Eddie saved my life." It was Eddie who, after Al died, said that "Jolson was the greatest performer of us all."

When the movie *The Jolson Story* had such a resounding success, it was the year for reminiscent old-men jokes in Hollywood. Eddie Cantor, his friend and rival, was especially aggressive about using them. Listening to Cantor hold forth one day, Jolson made the whispered aside, "One more stand-up joke about me, and I'll knock him down!"

When we were on radio together for two years, Al used to get a fan letter every week from some girl in Texas, a complete stranger. She kept listening to the show and criticizing it in a constructive way. He generally followed her advice, too.

The show was on the air during the 1948 Presidential campaign. The polls were predicting that Dewey would win, but Al was one of the few who didn't believe it. He sang "I'm Just Wild About Harry" on the preelection program.

Jolson had several wives. After his long sickness, he married his nurse, a girl named Erle. She was pale and transparent at the time, like a ghost that has materialized out of the air. After Jolson died, she married writer Norman Krasna. The last time

I saw her, she looked in the pink of health, a beautiful woman and a very nice person in every sense.

As Sainte-Beuve, the nineteenth-century French critic, said, most careers last fifteen years. It is a generalized statement about creative talent, but I would call it a pretty fair average. The show people I have just mentioned are of course the exception to the rule. And Judy Garland, at this moment of writing, is in the throes of another of her comebacks. Talent has to be practiced or else it will dissipate. Judy seems to do both; she has had more ups and downs than a scuba diver.

The so-called fickle public does not seem to apply to Judy. Her fans have remained loyal and steadfast, cheering her on with hysterical devotion whenever she rises to sing again. The annual showing of *The Wizard of Oz* on television helps, I am sure, to keep her in a state of perpetuity.

When she made the movie *A Star Is Born* with James Mason, it was Pamela Mason who said, "Judy can only sing for nothing." It was almost true. At parties, Judy would sing all night, endlessly; nothing could stop her; but when it came time to appear on a movie set she just wouldn't show up.

I don't know the nature of Judy's neurosis, but she and I have a few similar symptoms of stage fright. When she was married to director Vincente Minnelli she had her first brief bout with psychiatry. Her analyst sent her to Stockbridge, and she came back breathing fire. She was taking paraldehyde, and you could smell it a suburb away. Her analyst also advised Arthur Freed not to have Judy and Vincente work together. Vincente, who had directed two of Judy's pictures, *Meet Me in St. Louis* and *The Clock,* was preparing her next one, *Easter Parade.* He was taken off the picture and replaced by Chuck Walters.

Because of the analyst's advice, Vincente didn't work for two and a half years. He was eventually rescued from oblivion by producer Pandro S. Berman for the film *Madame Bovary.* After his divorce from Judy, he directed two of the great ones, *American in Paris* and *Gigi*.

Vincente Minelli and I have a relationship like that between Charlie Chaplin and a drunk in one of his movies, *City Lights*. (A rich man loved the little tramp when he was drunk and didn't know him when he was sober.) Vincente and I see each other, mostly when he's between wives. We discovered that the best time to see movies is four o'clock on a Sunday afternoon. After the showing of one foreign film, *The Silence,* Vincente asked: "What did you think of that autoeroticism scene?"

I had missed it—too busy reading the subtitles!

When Judy Garland was married to Sid Luft, she used to come to my house several afternoons a week, on some pretext or other, and ask me for sleeping pills. I would always give her two, and every time I did it I would say the same damned phrase that would haunt me later, "This doesn't solve anything, Judy."

She came in the evening and showed great skill in purloining pills. She'd excuse herself from the living room and disappear. I'd think she'd gone to my wife's room, but she'd go to my bathroom—where I had smokestacks of pills—and empty half the bottles. My wife was suspicious right away.

When I was in similar despairing situations and no longer had access to pills, I'd get to the guest bathroom medicine cabinet in other people's houses on the slightest pretext. But my wife had usually phoned ahead of time and they'd hidden their pills.

On one occasion when Judy and I embraced each other, I felt that it was such a unification of two great pill repositories it must have been a peak in pharmaceutical history. If Judy and I had married, she would have given birth to a sleeping pill instead of a child—we could have named it Barb-Iturate.

When Judy had her weekly television shows in 1963, I said,

"She's a vibrato in search of a voice." It doesn't seem to matter when she plays the Palace, however—she can do no wrong as far as her devotees are concerned.

When Judy grew up on the MGM lot she was surrounded by such beauties as Lana Turner, Ava Gardner, and Elizabeth Taylor. For a throbbingly emotional girl, she must have felt overshadowed, not as far as talent was concerned—she always had that—but in other areas. She was the cute kid who never grew up, yet she grew increasingly harder to handle. On her account, directors were fired or replaced, and it is reported that at the finish of one movie she jumped in her car and in a fury tried to run over the director.

The last time I saw Judy, it was at a New Year's Eve party. She recited from memory a letter I had written to her many years ago. I remembered—it was a reply to a letter of hers—she had had a schoolgirl crush. But she was Andy Hardy's girl friend then, and I was the terror of radio.

The newest member to join this exalted group of superstars is Barbra Streisand. (I was going to say the newest contender for the throne, but she's already on it.)

I cannot remember any star as young as she is, possessing the stage presence, vocal control, and quality as well as the truly original style that is the mark of a great performer. As an actress and a singer she can be funny as well as touching, sing a song with strength and be seemingly nerveless. She learned early the most important and the rarest thing of all—not to be a carbon copy and to allow her own personality to emerge. No doubt about it, she has joined the illustrious few who have cast a whole new mold. Her meteoric rise and unusual appearance have paved the way for others; unpretty girls with good singing voices now abound in the land.

She lives in Beverly Hills, a stone's throw away from me. (In my condition I couldn't throw a pebble.) In a lavish home, with servants, baby nurse, secretary, etc., and with a formidable butler from the Aly Khan type of school, Barbra endeared herself to a listener when she remarked apologetically, "This is all too new to me not to be intimidated by the help." She knows that underneath it all she's not really a Rothschild. Not yet anyway.

The cultural descent of the United States can be spelled out by musical instruments. First, the popularity of the ukulele, then the banjo, and finally the guitar.

I talked recently to a female friend of mine who considers herself an expert on modern popular music. She said to me: "Bobby Dylan is the new Jesus Christ." She did not laugh—or even smile—as she said it. I looked closely, but she seemed to be serious. I am aware of the fact that the two legends of the rock age are Bob Dylan and the Beatles. But Elvis Presley, let us not forget, started the whole thing. It hardly seems possible that old Swivel Hips was considered so unfit for human eyes that Ed Sullivan refused to let him be shown in his entirety—only his face was allowed on camera. Elvis now seems pretty tame stuff, compared to the wild and abandoned go-go swingers and discotheque dancers of today. Anyway, it all has a surgical effect on me—it makes me want to cut my throat.

The tempo of modern music in the popular field often confuses me. I know it is necessary to vary it to maintain interest, but the other night I listened to Andy Williams—a very good singer, by the way—render Jerome Kern's "The Way You Look Tonight." He sang it so slowly that I could not figure out how he remembered the words from phrase to phrase.

I do not even know when the word "operetta" disappeared. That automatically brings up Sigmund Romberg. Not too long ago, Pamela Mason told me flatly that she preferred Romberg to Brahms. I got up and walked out. I don't know how one can account for tastes like that.

In the thirties, I was a member of a network radio orchestra conducted by Sigmund Romberg. For one particular program I was scheduled to play the first four bars of the *Moonlight Sonata*. It was an easy thing to do, so I didn't give it a thought. During the performance, and to my absolute horror, I hit a wrong note in the second bar. These triplets are so exposed and the piece is so familiar that the mistake was apparent to everyone. I was mortified beyond belief, and what's more Romberg fired me.

Last year, Artur Rubinstein, the great virtuoso, gave a recital at Carnegie Hall. He opened his program with the *Moonlight Sonata*. He hit a clinker in the second bar. Need I say that I laughed like hell?

On the other end of the musical spectrum, I was partly responsible for Benny Goodman's first job as a bandleader. It was at the Café de Paree in the middle thirties; I sold Billy Rose on the idea. Up to that time, Benny had been an outstanding jazz clarinetist in a very good pit orchestra that backed the production of *Girl Crazy* in 1930. Benny became the first bandleader to integrate an orchestra—with Teddy Wilson at the piano and Lionel Hampton at the vibraphone. The band used to call him "the man with the X-ray eyes." He was very strict, a harsh taskmaster. He was also a moody and inarticulate person. I was reminded of his lack of volubility when I read a newspaper account of his meeting with the Beatles. It seems that when the Beatles played in Forest Hills, Long Island, arrangements were made so that Benny Goodman could bring his daughter to meet them. At the meeting Ringo said to the former King of Swing: "We have an old seventy-eight record of yours."

Benny said, "Oh."

That was all. Silence on both sides.

According to the report, the generation gap was never more apparent.

Teddy Wilson, who had played with the Goodman band, was an untutored jazz pianist with a natural dazzling technique. One of the differences between jazz and classical pianism is a light and feathery touch as opposed to a deep and sonorous tone.

When I heard that Teddy had started formal piano study, I strongly advised him against it. Years later, I heard that Leonard Bernstein had given him the same advice.

Unfortunately, Teddy continued his studies, and when I next heard him play, the lightness had gone and the technique was marred.

The great jazz pianist and songwriter Fats Waller—"Ain't Misbehavin'" and "Honeysuckle Rose"—had what was called a great left hand (they don't use left hands in jazz anymore). For an organ concert that he gave at Carnegie Hall he billed himself as THE BLACK HOROWITZ.

And while we are on the subject, it should be remembered that Fletcher Henderson, a bandleader, jazz pianist, and orchestrator of unique talent, wrote many of Benny Goodman's orchestrations. His contributions are often overlooked by jazz historians.

Before the thirties, the ability to orchestrate was a rather rare talent. Ragtime, with all its demands, was followed by jazz—not the improvisations but the written music—and the big bands commenced to dominate the musical scene. Good orchestrators followed the demand and became quite common.

I want to mention two fine bandsmen in particular—Jean Goldkette and Ben Pollack—because they brought something wonderfully new in popular music. Music became really big business. It sprouted all sorts of offshoots. Jules Stein, now head of the show biz conglomerate called MCA, Inc., told me that he used to play violin around Chicago. He got his multi-millionaire start booking bands in that area. Meyer Davis, the society bandleader of those times, appeared from nowhere. He once backed a play of George S. Kaufman's and timidly offered a suggestion. I never saw the glance that withers in any better form than the one which George gave him.

Once I sat in for a week as fill-in pianist for Paul Whiteman and his orchestra when Bing Crosby was singing for him. At the time, I remember, I was having a wild affair with a great and married movie star. I used to play with Whiteman, listen to Bing and the Rhythm Boys, then rush back to my hotel to sit and wait for the phone to ring.

The affair went on for two months after I left Whiteman. It finally ended, and perhaps it was all for the best. As a married acquaintance of mine, who had gone through a similar experience, remarked, "The worst part of having a mistress is those two dinners you have to eat."

Which reminds me of an old Viennese joke. It was about the young musician who had just made love to his second girl of the evening. He got up and hastily put on his clothes.

"Where are you going?" demanded the girl.

"Down to the coffeehouse to tell everybody," he said.

It is a typical Viennese story.

Joey Bushkin is a jazz pianist from the old days. When he told me he had a great pill collection, as an old and revered pill collector, I asked to see them. He proudly showed them to me ensconced in a silver box. I was never more contemptuous of anything in my life. He had only three or four really good pills: only a couple were rare, and very few were vintage. The rest were simply different kinds of tranquilizers.

I met Joey later at a wedding reception at the home of Groucho Marx. Each of us was convinced that the other must carry his pills around with him. So we immediately started a period of collective bargaining. Groucho came over to us and said: "If I'd known that you two were going to show up today, I could have saved the expense of hiring a piano player!"

"We're not pianists," I said desperately. "We're pharmacists!"

If anyone ever does a musical of my life, he has my permission to call it *Trauma Boy.*

Chapter 3

I CAN do no worse than quote some comments about me made by the eminent English drama critic Kenneth Tynan. He visited this country in 1954. He went back to write about me in a spring issue of the magazine *Punch*. In his own fashion he faithfully reported the meeting.

"Oscar Levant, pianist and wit," he wrote, "whose face awake bears expression of utter disgust most men wear asleep. Am put in mind, uncharitably, of squashed bicycle saddle. Pearl is disease of oyster: Levant is disease of Hollywood."

As if this were not enough, Tynan heaped outrage on obloquy:

Slouching sickly about room, he announces: "People either dislike or detest me." I try out faint smile, which he interprets as personal insult. "You have a big guilt quotient, don't you?" he says invitingly, with deep intestinal chuckle, going on to discuss weaknesses of Berlioz and Schubert very intelligently but with ferocious and unsubtle display of Lifemanship. Further conversation impaired by warning from friend that should anyone mention Prokofiev's Third Piano Concerto, Levant leaves the room never to return. Nervously bring up subject of piano, whither he lunges: "What'll it be, kids? A Stabat Mater or a blues?"

Tynan also told one of the private stock of bellicose stories about me:

As he plays, friend tells story of occasion when son-in-law of studio head heard Levant playing "Lady, Play Your Mandolin" (only popular song he ever wrote) and said: "That's right, Oscar. Play us a medley of your hit." Slamming the keyboard, Levant bellowed back: "O.K.—play us a medley of your father-in-law!" He leaves well before midnight, grimacing and explaining that he must catch up on usual twenty-two hours of sleep. Undeniably, a powerful soul.

The trouble with this is that with the exception of the father-in-law line it is almost entirely apocryphal. Tynan was just a precocious young man in those days. For one thing, I have written many popular songs. They may not have been ''standards," but several were hits of the time. (The most popular, "Blame It on My Youth," brings back more memories than royalties.)

The place of that first meeting with Kenneth Tynan had been in Beverly Hills at the home of the Ira Gershwins. I was not aware that he was a critic—and not informed that he would use the occasion to write a piece about me.

A tall, slender young man with an elongated face (his own description: the reflection in a spoon), a slight stammer, and a transparent skin that could turn crimson with emotion, Tynan indulged in lavish blandishments to the ladies. In answer to my wife's polite query as to whether or not he liked Southern

California, he soulfully replied that he liked it a great deal better since he had met her. (He had *just* met her.) To Vera Zorina, on the occasion of their first meeting: "I have been watching you for the past fifteen minutes, and they have been the most fascinating fifteen minutes of my life!"

Tynan, an Oxford graduate, had made an early effort to be an actor. His performance in a play with Alec Guinness got him a bad review. In rebuttal, he wrote to the editor a brilliant open letter that gained him a job as theater critic for the same paper. That started his career.

A disciple of the late English critic James Agate, Tynan eventually became drama critic for one of the world's leading newspapers, the weekly London *Observer*. There he flourished. In my opinion, he was the most brilliant critic in the English-speaking language. (In spite of his obsession with the plays of Bertolt Brecht.)

He also became known as one of England's "angry young men." The catalyst for this emotion was John Osborne's anti-establishment play *Look Back in Anger*. Conservative critics blasted the play as a social outrage; Somerset Maugham described the characters as "scum." But Tynan's defense and praise struck a response in a generation fed up with stale traditions. The work was a major breakthrough. Personally, I liked the play even though the intolerable fury was hard for me to endure.

I hated Osborne's *The Entertainer* the first time I saw it. Some friends persuaded me that I was mistaken. So I saw it again, and I hated it again. All except for one line: "Better a has-been than a never-was." On second thought, I cannot say I really like it; at my age, it is a very hard line to take.

Kenneth Tynan came to this country in the late fifties to be the theater critic for the *New Yorker* magazine—a post he held for two years. Although his overall estimate of the New York theater was rather dim, he was eminently readable and controversial. The reason that he turned down the same position for the exalted New York *Times* was that he could not function at his best with the pressure of a daily deadline review. He resumed reviewing for the *Observer* until the Chichester Theatre, which became the National Theatre, was formed. Tynan then gave up theater criticism in order to become associated with Laurence Olivier in that notable venture.

I came to know Tynan better in the years that followed his survey of me. At one period in his stormy marriage to the novelist Elaine Dundy, he confided that he had gone to a psychoanalyst to find out why he stayed married to her. Figuratively speaking, they constantly rubbed broken glass in each other's eyes when they were wed.

At another time Tynan returned to Los Angeles as the representative of a television show for the British Broadcasting Corporation. The program had to do with American eccentrics in public life. Naturally, he visited me to persuade me to be a guest. I was not interested in appearing on a show with a lot of oddballs. Even if I did qualify.

Tynan is a good mimic—he does a great imitation of Noel Coward's clipped accent. Noel had just appeared in a revival of G. B. Shaw's *The Apple Cart*. I asked Tynan his opinion of Coward's acting. He said: "He's good in sentences, but not in paragraphs." I thought it was an astute judgment. Coward always says each stage sentence perfectly—and each one in the same way. Perhaps that is why his dialogue is usually one-sentence stuff.

Nor does Tynan care much for T. S. Eliot as a playwright. He delivered the *coup de grâce* to Eliot's play *The Elder Statesman* by stating at the end of his review that it was "pure Noel Coward." In Tynan's lexicon, he could have said nothing worse.

Tynan is always careful to write and speak so that he is quotable. I liked his comment about C. P. Snow, the English scientist and novelist who is now a politician. Speaking of one of Snow's plays, he said: "Snow is not hard-driven." Tynan also revealed the secret of writing book-length manuscripts. "You just steal a little bit here and there," he said.

There appears to be a slight feud between Tynan and Terence Rattigan, the English playwright. Rattigan has written both bad and wonderful plays, but they are always dramatic. He is supposed to be the most wealthy of all the contemporary playwrights. That makes him quite wealthy. In spite of David Susskind's comment that "all Rattigan does is write a well-made play"—something that seems to me a basic accomplishment—Rattigan has had no trouble about success.

I like what he does. He wrote, for one, *The Winslow Boy.* I was told that the original idea for it was given Rattigan by Aneurin Bevan, the great darling of the British Left. Another of his plays, *The Browning Version,* was made into a touching movie. I saw it right after my heart attack and became very emotional about it. It is a prime example of an actor-proof drama. Of all the accomplished actors who played the title role, Eric Portman was Rattigan's favorite.

Two more of his plays that became movies were *The Deep Blue Sea* and *Separate Tables.* I think it is unusual that Rattigan is always able to produce this enormous emotional reaction in the audience—if one eliminates the crap in his plays that all playwrights have to use.

I was interested in Rattigan's reaction to Kenneth Tynan's review of his little-known play based on *Camille*—in which the characters are all male and homosexual. Tynan had reviewed it unfavorably for the London *Observer* and had ended with the extraordinary sentence, "After all, he needs me—I don't need him."

Rattigan got his revenge later. He wrote to Tynan, "Since you've been on the *New Yorker* you've slipped, and have become a big *bore!*"

❧   ❧   ❧

The first newspaper drama critic to write publicly about the well-known fact that the three leading playwrights of the American theater are homosexuals was Stanley Kauffmann, in an article for the New York *Times* about two years ago.

He cited the undeniable truth that the views of these writers on love, sex, and marriage stemmed from an insular and circumscribed point of view.

One prominent and intelligent lady that I know refuses to see plays by homosexual authors. She does not want to see life through the eyes of a writer who does not have a personal part in providing a future generation.

I have no understanding of the plight of the homosexual. As S. N. Behrman once wrote with some irritation: "Homosexuals are not the only ones that have problems."

The English National Theatre's production of Chekhov's *Uncle Vanya,* shown on American television in 1967, was flawlessly performed by Laurence Olivier, Michael Redgrave, Joan Plowright, Rosemary Harris, and Sybil Thorndike. My wife wanted to break the television set. What else could top it?

The first time I saw Chekhov's *The Sea Gull* was in the late thirties. The play as well as the cast, Alfred Lunt, Lynn Fontanne, and Uta Hagen, impressed me deeply.

There is a line in *The Sea Gull* that I found endearing. Chekhov gives Trigorin, the writer in his play, these words: "And when I'm dead they'll be saying at my grave, 'Here lies Trigorin, a delightful writer but not so good as Turgenev.'"

As a footnote, it may be interesting to mention that Chekhov's plays with their limited appeal have, over the years, sustained the same audience quotient. As opposed, that is, to other playwrights, Eugene O'Neill for example, who is revived every so often and then gets forgotten all over again.

The veterans of the theater have a special attraction for me. Many years ago in New York, I saw Laurette Taylor in a Long-

champs restaurant. She was sitting alone at a table and beck-
oned me over to her. I sat with her and tried to be comforting.
I knew her talent, and I also knew that she had not worked
for ten years.

Shortly after that she starred in *The Glass Menagerie* and
became a warm legend in theater history. That was the play
at which the author, Tennessee Williams, nearly went crazy on
opening night. He could have spared himself the trouble.

I also met the veteran English actress, Dame Edith Evans, at
Sardi's. She was seated at a table with Ruth Gordon, another
longtime actress.

I mentioned to Dame Edith that I remembered her performance in *Lady of the Lamp,* a story of Florence Nightingale.

"What year was that?" I asked.

"I believe it was 1937," replied Dame Edith.

"1932," said Ruth Gordon promptly.

I have great respect for the genuine old-timers.

In 1958 Ethel Barrymore would send me piano requests, via
her son Sammy Colt, to play on my weekly TV show. The music
she preferred was usually Bach.

I should mention, too, that out of all the Hollywood colony,
it was only Katharine Hepburn who visited Ethel as often as
possible, right up to her death. I agree with Scott Fitzgerald's
line, "I like Katharine Hepburn in anything."

If Judith Anderson does not stop doing *Medea!* She has done
this remarkable adaptation by Robinson Jeffers so long and so
well that she has almost become a Greek witch herself. She also
does it so perfectly that it seems easy. I recall seeing one of her
performances and coming out to hear a chorus girl—who had
never been on the stage in her life except as a "statuesque
beauty"—remark to her escort: "*I* would have played it differently."

There are less charitable views of actresses. One was that of the veteran critic, author, and caricaturist, Max Beerbohm, who, when he was advanced in years, was asked what he had thought of Eleanora Duse.

"She was terrible," he said.

"But what about when she was younger?" persisted the interviewer.

"She was worse," said Beerbohm. "She had more energy then."

It is worth noting here that a critic of the stature of Beerbohm always thought that theater was the least of literary practices. "Had I been told that I was destined to write about plays for twelve weeks," he said in a farewell essay in 1910, "I should have shuddered. Had I been told that I was destined to write about them for twelve years, I should have expired on the spot, neatly falsifying the prediction." He added: "I do not recall that I have once sat down eager to write or that I have once written with ease and delight." But he admitted that this was not due entirely to his theme but to the fact that he had "an acute literary conscience."

Max Beerbohm succeeded George Bernard Shaw as a drama critic for the English literary magazine of the nineties, the *Saturday Review*. Shaw's last line for that publication had been: Next week the incomparable Max.

The affection of the two men for each other had been marred when Beerbohm's half brother, Beerbohm Tree, played the role of Professor Higgins in Shaw's play *Pygmalion*. Shaw and the actor disliked each other and argued continually. Max, on the other hand, adored his older brother and made it an ethical point never to review his shows.

As a matter of historical fact, Beerbohm Tree was more than a half brother to Max Beerbohm. They had the same father, and their mothers were sisters. While you figure that out, I must also add the information that the name Beerbohm means tree in German. Beerbohm Tree's rightful name was Herbert Beerbohm; he had dropped the Herbert and added Tree.

Pygmalion, called a "potboiler" by Shaw, had been written as a vehicle for the actress Mrs. Pat Campbell, with whom he was in love. (In their well-publicized exchange of letters she referred to herself and Shaw as "passionless lions.")

Incidentally, the story of Pygmalion (which is really the story of Galatea) is one of the most resuscitated dramatic works in history. It was done by the Greeks, the Romans, the English, the Americans—and possibly some others—in various versions. Even W. S. Gilbert wrote a play about the incident in the 1880's.

Gilbert, the waspish member of the Gilbert and Sullivan team, had little regard for the acting ability of Sir Beerbohm Tree. He felt that the controversy over the true identity of Shakespeare could be settled once and for all. His solution was to have Beerbohm Tree recite from the Bard over the graves of the three contenders, Shakespeare, Bacon, and Marlowe. The real Shakespeare would, he felt certain, turn in his grave.

At a Hollywood soiree a few years back, I met Iris Tree, the daughter of Beerbohm Tree. A charming and witty woman, she told me the surprising news that she had accompanied her father to Hollywood in 1915 when he had starred in a silent movie of *Macbeth.* (It was so bad it was never released.) Tree was also the founder of the renowned London Academy of Dramatic Art.

Gene Tunney, the heavyweight champion fighter, was sometimes on the radio show *Information Please* with me. His hobby was Shakespeare, and he would recite interminably. But the story about Tunney which appeals to me most does not concern the ring. It happened when he went to London and met Max Beerbohm. In the course of the visit Tunney had elaborately and pretentiously described a sunset. After the visit,

Beerbohm said, "I had to steel every nerve in my body to meet such sensitivity."

S. N. Behrman, the distinguished contemporary playwright, is the author of a book of conversations and reminiscences about Max Beerbohm. For the preparation of the book, Sam had many interviews with his friend Max. Although he was not permitted to take notes, he captured the Beerbohm style to perfection. Beerbohm revealed to him that his friend Oscar Wilde had been a physically powerful man. That startled me—my own idea of Wilde had always been that he was on the effeminate side. I forget who informed me, but one of the stories I heard about Oscar Wilde was that his favorite song was "The London Derriere."

The revivals of George Bernard Shaw are becoming almost as rhythmic as the seasons in London and on Broadway. Next to Shakespeare, he is the most revived author—but I must say he always expected it to be that way. His self-assurance was a trial to those who knew him. It was again Oscar Wilde who remarked that "Shaw has no enemies but he is heartily disliked by all his friends." Ironically enough, as a young man Shaw had doubts about everything, including himself.

Nevertheless, he had a considerable share of that intuition which marks a great artist. When he wrote his *Apple Cart*—which described the plight of a king bereft of power who runs for election as member of Parliament—he got a letter from the exiled Kaiser Wilhelm in Doorn. It praised him for his political perspicacity.

I relish the short snappers by Shaw. One of his plays was turned down for years by a certain producer. At last, after Shaw was famous, he cabled him an offer for production. Shaw cabled back: BETTER NEVER THAN LATE.

The Theatre Guild once cabled him for permission to make

a cut in one of his lengthy plays. Otherwise, they informed him, commuters would miss their trains.

"Change the train schedules," was Shaw's solution.

About Albert Einstein, whose hobby was the violin, Shaw said, "He's the only violinist who *looks* like a violinist."

Which reminds me that Albert Einstein liked to play with a string quartet when he was living in Princeton, New Jersey. After a private performance, one of the violinists complained, "He can't count!"

After Shaw's death, his secretary of many years, Blanche Patch, wrote a book about her experiences with the great man. One critic commented, "Only G.B.S. would have had a humourless secretary."

I asked Kenneth Tynan whom he preferred as a drama critic, Shaw or Beerbohm. His choice was Shaw.

David Belasco, a Western-born impresario and playwright, wrote the libretto for *Girl of the Golden West,* an opera by Puccini. That was in 1910, and it was a failure. The 1966 revival was a big New York hit. Belasco was always derided as "corny" and antiquated, yet his devices have survived. One of his earliest plays, given in London in 1898, received a good review by the discerning Shaw.

"*The Heart of Maryland* is not a bad specimen of the American machine-made melodrama," wrote Shaw. And about the star: "Mrs. Leslie Carter is a melodramatic heroine of no mean powers. Her dresses and graces and poses cast a glamor of high art on Mr. Belasco's romance." The word "glamor" by Shaw is a surprise to me. I always thought it came into public usage around the advent of Marlene Dietrich.

When the actress Mrs. Leslie Carter was sued for divorce, her husband was supposed to have named over thirty corespondents. Evidently "glamor" can have its problems.

The Hecht-MacArthur play *Twentieth Century* was in large

part pure hoke derived from the antics of the flamboyant David Belasco and his son-in-law, Morris Gest (an impresario for imported European spectacles). It was directed by Jed Harris, who was responsible for refining many of the Belasco techniques.

As often as I could, in the old days of boxing, I went to see the bouts in Madison Square Garden. I liked the atmosphere as much as the fights. Belasco, who always wore a turned-back collar like a priest, was famous for his Friday night attendance —usually with some ingenue that he was currently courting. He always had two seats ringside. The week after his death these two seats were kept empty. Just before the fight, for a minute or so, they turned a spotlight on them. I told this to Cathleen Nesbitt, the veteran actress who worked with Belasco. She said: "David would have loved it; it is so hammy."

It is strange to look back and see all the theater talents that line up behind the years. In the twenties the Russian producer-director Constantin Stanislavsky and the German (Austrian-born) producer-director Max Reinhardt brought their productions to New York to great acclaim and kudos.

Reinhardt's productions were usually extravagant spectacles like *A Midsummer Night's Dream* (he also directed the movie version), *Danton's Death, Everyman,* and *The Miracle.* I also recall his production of a Tolstoi play, *The Living Corpse,* that starred the great European actor, Alexander Moise.

The mention of Max Reinhardt's name recalls a story told me by Gottfried Reinhardt, the son of Max. Gottfried, a fledgling director, had fled Europe and Hitler in 1933, arriving penniless in New York. He had the prospect of a job as elevator boy at the Columbia Broadcasting Studios when, through an influential friend with access to the great houses, he was brought to dinner at the home of William S. Paley, the head of CBS. Naturally, Gottfried's plight was not known to the host or his guests, some of the richest people in New York.

It so happened that the dinner took place on the night that President Roosevelt declared his unprecedented bank holiday. After dinner, Paley noted that the emergency measure could prove quite an inconvenience. "If anyone needs cash, I have it," he added. The only one who took advantage of his kind offer was Gottfried. He asked for five hundred. He got it, too.

Stanislavsky's legendary Moscow Art Theatre set New York on its ear when the company appeared there in 1923. The acting technique employed by the company was a system devised by Stanislavsky, the same system that was later to be known as "the method." Actors Akim Tamiroff and Michael Chekhov, nephew of the dramatist, were closely associated with the company, the latter in the capacity of director and teacher.

1950 was the year that I met the Russian Juri Jelagin, when I played with the Houston Symphony in Birmingham, Alabama. Jelagin, a violinist with the orchestra, had written a definitive firsthand account of the decline of the arts in Russia during the thirties. From this book, *The Taming of the Arts,* I learned of the tragic story of Vsevolod Meyerhold, one of the biggest stage directors in Russia.

In 1937 Meyerhold was in artistic exile, along with the composer Dimitri Shostakovich. No one in the theatrical world could get employment without the sanction of Stalin's officials.

As a young man, Meyerhold was a student of Stanislavsky, then he became a director for the imperial theater. One of the first artists to join the Communist party after the Revolution, he had his own theater where his modern innovations won for him worldwide attention.

His next to last production before his banishment had been *Camille,* with his actress-wife in the leading role. The presentation of the play was a departure from his usual modern technique. Authentic Second Empire furniture decorated the sets; even the smallest props were genuine antiques. It was a great hit with the audience, but the Soviet propaganda committee, ever on the lookout for "decadence" in art, was displeased. Because of this and other alleged infractions, the Meyerhold Theatre was liquidated. The Moscow Art Theatre of Stanislavsky had already been abolished.

Although Shostakovich had been restored to favor because of his majestic Fifth Symphony, Meyerhold was not as fortunate. He was given a public hearing in 1939 in order to recant. To be taken off the blacklist, he was expected to renounce his former creative efforts.

The elderly and disenchanted Meyerhold made his scheduled public appearance. Instead of an abject false confession, he eloquently defended himself and his works, denouncing the prevailing Socialistic realism theater as worthless. He concluded his "apology" by accusing the committee of destroying art.

Meyerhold was arrested and was never heard of again. His wife was brutally murdered. The era of the creative Russian theater had come to an end.

In the early thirties, the Group Theatre, composed of actors, directors, and playwrights, was the first American acting company to study the Stanislavsky system. The original members included John Garfield, Lee Cobb, Franchot Tone, Stella and Luther Adler, Morris Carnovsky, Clifford Odets, Harold Clurman, Elia Kazan, and Lee Strasberg.

Clifford Odets' first play, *Awake and Sing,* was not too heartily endorsed by the New York *Times* critic Brooks Atkinson. When it was later revived, Atkinson was more impressed. He said to director Harold Clurman, "The play has changed."

"No," replied Harold. "You have."

Harold Clurman became a leading director and producer as well as an excellent drama critic. His book *The Fervent Years* was, and is, the definitive history of the Group Theatre.

Harold's marriage to the actress Stella Adler produced a few choice remarks. Her admonition, "Stop sleeping like a great man!" became quite well known. When their marriage broke up, the story goes, she took all of their mutual possessions. When he asked, "What are you leaving for me?" she dramatically threw open the curtains and pointed to the lights below. "I am leaving you all of Broadway," she replied.

Over the years the Group gradually disbanded, hastened by the Hollywood success of several of its members. Others of the alumni formed drama workshops, among them Stella Adler. Lee Strasberg became the director of the Actors Studio.

In 1947 Marlon Brando (a pupil of Stella Adler) created such an enormous impact with his performance in *A Streetcar Named Desire* (directed by Elia Kazan) that he was catapulted into the role of a theatrical innovator. He synthesized a new era, that of the method actor.

Elia Kazan, one of the cofounders of the Actors Studio, had developed from a unique actor into the most successful director on Broadway. He has the unprecedented record of directing five Pulitzer Prize dramas. I attended the first play that he directed, *Casey Jones* by Robert Ardrey. It didn't make it. However, the chemistry between Kazan and Tennessee Williams produced magic results; the four plays that they did together were brilliant.

Kazan's direction of the Arthur Miller play *Death of a Salesman* was another of his triumphs. Kazan had an ideological break with Arthur Miller, and their differences were never resolved, even when he directed *After the Fall.* Kazan is one of the prototypes in Arthur Miller's biographical drama. In *After the Fall,* this dramatic self-love affair, the explicable becomes trite and humor is carefully avoided. I must add, however, that there is an excellent scene at the end of the first act, when the prototype of Arthur Miller meets the prototype of Marilyn Monroe in Central Park. It is the best scene in the play, true to pseudolife. In the second act, the self-revelatory catharsis of "Marilyn" bored me. Taking away the blond wig and the stupidity, I kept thinking of Judy Garland.

As for the general tone of his public statements, Arthur Miller, whom I call Mr. Doomsday, obviously expects the world to end momentarily. He will no doubt see to it that he is the only one to survive.

The well-publicized association of Marilyn Monroe with the Actors Studio focused public attention on the Lee Strasberg workshop. Paul Newman is also an outstanding product of the Actors Studio. Around 1955 or so, I saw him in the Broadway play *The Desperate Hours*. After the show we exchanged a few words at Sardi's. Several months later I encountered him at a Hollywood party, looking shy and out of it. He had come West to make a movie, but did not expect to stay any longer than necessary. "Too close to the cake," he grinned. "Also no place to study," he added.

Paul Newman's step-by-step success—movies, plus stage plays, plus study—accounts, I am sure, for his present high position as a solid (and "bankable") star. The only other young American star with equal international rating is Steve McQueen.

It was at Downey's, a restaurant frequented by actors, that I met Kim Stanley, the Goddess of the Method. I had just taped a *Jack Parr* show and had mentioned that I thought she should win an award for her performance on a *Ben Casey* television show. She did win when the time came around, but that's not the point of my story.

On the night that I met her I said enthusiastically, "That was the best thing you've ever done!"

She looked irritated. "You cannot be very familiar with my work if you say that," she replied. She indignantly went on to enumerate the difficulties she had faced on the television show—the early hours, the lack of preparation, the rush for time, etc. Okay! All I had done was pay her a compliment.

A dramatist, who shall be nameless, has observed that Kim Stanley is a "gifted amateur." Meaning, I suppose, that she is not the-show-must-go-on type of performer. It has also been claimed that no matter what role she plays, she wants the sympathy of the audience. That seems to me a minor complaint.

The truth is, she is a remarkable actress, and certainly the most feminine of the lot.

When she was turned down by Edward Albee for the London company of *Who's Afraid of Virginia Woolf?* because he thought she was too soft and gentle for the part, she said in a printed interview that she was quite disappointed. "Why must the part be played by a dike?" she asked frankly. It was in the staid New York *Times,* too.

I see by the papers that Julie Harris has finally gotten around to playing Blanche in *A Streetcar Named Desire.* She joins the lustrous ranks of notable actresses who have played Tennessee Williams' tragic heroine.

It was Jessica Tandy who played the original Blanche DuBois. Uta Hagen also enacted the role, and I understand that her interpretation was about the most touching of all. When Kim Stanley played the part—in the city of Dallas, I believe—I heard that she became so immersed in the character that she had trouble shaking it off when she left the theater.

Most of the time an actress who fufills the demands of a difficult role finds the satisfaction derived from her professional accomplishment a stimulating rather than a depressing experience. This is sometimes hard for an average theater-goer to understand.

I remember when Uta Hagen created the exhausting role of Martha in *Who's Afraid of Virginia Woolf?* I glimpsed her after the show at Sardi's as she sat calmly enjoying her supper. Members of the audience who had witnessed her powerful performance were almost too unnerved to eat.

The late Vivien Leigh also portrayed Blanche in the London company of *Streetcar,* and not to very good notices either. Kenneth Tynan in particular thought she was completely miscast. And he also dubbed the direction of Laurence Olivier as clumsy. It is, therefore, cheering to remember that Vivien Leigh not only won the role in the movie but also received an Academy Award for her efforts.

Apropos of all of this, I can only say that I have appointed myself the President of the Blanche DuBois Club.

In the war years, writers took the issues of the day very seriously. Henri Bernstein, the French playwright who had his own theater, fled France at the onset of World War II. He slapped the English playwright, Frederick Lonsdale, in the face at a restaurant in New York. He felt that Lonsdale was pro-Fascist.

Bernstein was always high-spirited. As a young man he even had a duel with another Frenchman, Édouard Bourdet, the author of *The Captive.*

In the forties I met Henri Bernstein at the home of Herbert Bayard Swope. A man of seventy, Bernstein was De Gaulle tall, vigorous, and zestful, with definite opinions and an eye for the ladies. My wife and I had only been married a few weeks when he said to her roguishly in his Charles Boyer accent, "Are you still faithful?" She replied in the affirmative. "Well, if things should change," he said hopefully, "think of me."

There is no question that in the twenties the most successful playwright in the world was Ferenc Molnár. Molnár was always very handsome. When he came to New York from Europe, he fell in love with a rather young girl. It was a wonderful romance, and when she died unexpectedly it was a tragic situation. Molnár wrote many hit plays and several novels, of which *The Paul Street Boys* was my favorite.

I remember in the forties that Leonard Lyons, the columnist for the New York *Post,* gave a dinner party for Molnár, and I was invited. Leonard tells the story about that evening at his home. After dinner his son demonstrated his piano lessons for us, and Molnár made up a little story about it.

"The neighbors see Oscar Levant enter this apartment," he said, "and they wait and listen. They are rewarded by hearing the piano playing. They nod to each other and say, 'No doubt Oscar is playing one of those new twelve-tone pieces by Schoenberg. A very brilliant pianist, that Oscar.'"

Leonard Lyons has always been a kindly, sentimental adherent of the great. He was the keeper of the eccentric Irish roustabout playwright Brendan Behan, when he arrived in New York. Behan dubbed Lyons "the friend of the immigrant."

Another Irish playwright, Sean O'Casey, when he came to New York was the private fief of drama critic George Jean Nathan. I met O'Casey at the old Stork Club, Nathan's favorite hangout. Nathan was in love with Lillian Gish for years in a wild platonic way; then he fell in love with her alter ego, the equally fragile and evanescent Julie Haydon. I used to try to talk to him, but he was always so sloshed that I never could get sense out of him.

Once I used a line that I thought was original: When I can't sleep, I read a book by Steve Allen. My wife June, who has become the authority on literature in our family, then told me that Sean O'Casey had used the line first in one of his one-act plays. His character declared: "When I can't sleep, I read a book by William Butler Yeats."

I witnessed the antics of Richard Burton in his interpretation of *Hamlet* by a famous English author whose name escapes me. He was so vigorous and healthy that I can say positively it is the only version in which the audience feels sorry for Claudius. As I heard Hamlet beg his mother to assume a virtue if she had it not, my memory went back to my old high school teacher. That's the line she pulled on me when she wanted me to be a gentleman.

Richard Burton's fine resonant voice has been described, at

least by one critic, as the voice of the century. Burton, on the other hand, has declared that for certain poetry his preference is the voice of John Gielgud. "That beautiful, artificial voice is unbeatable," was his comment. Burton's well-known devotion to poetry and liquor was influenced, according to him, by his early upbringing and his Welsh father.

One of the more famous English actors, who has worked both in New York and Hollywood, in due time came up for knighthood. Scotland Yard prepared its dossier on him, and the actor was called in for an interview. He was questioned about his sexual proclivities, and he solemnly promised: "I'll never do it again."

A week after he was awarded the honor, he was picked up by the police. He explained, "I was a naughty boy." Privately, he complained, "You can't do anything in England if you're a knight."

But that problem seems to confuse everyone. I used to know a charming homosexual actor who later became a director. He married a show girl and made a brave attempt to go straight, but he was always in the kitchen, cooking wonderful goodies. It was delightful for the guests. "Your husband certainly knows how to cook," one of them remarked to the wife.

"Yes," she replied wistfully. "If he could only fuck. . . ."

One actor I know talks incessantly, endlessly, boringly, his conversation a rondo of clichés. He is a one-man telethon, without a penny going to charity.

A producer was caught by his wife in a compromising situation with an actress. "I was just on the verge of getting her signature on a contract," he explained.

I was at a New Year's Eve party when a well-known Broadway actor boasted that in three years of woman-poaching in New York he had made forty-seven conquests.

"If you're going to keep records on how many hits you

made," I said irritably, "how about keeping tab on your strike-outs?"

Once when I discussed sex with a beautiful actress, she told me how frightening it was, at least the first time. "Yes," I said, recalling my stage experiences, "it's like New Haven, Philadelphia, and then New York."

Chapter 4

$\mathcal{I}$ HAVE no idea what wit is. I have no desire to discuss it. As André Maurois, the French biographer, said: "Analyzing wit is like dissecting a frog. When you take it apart you find out what it is made of, but the subject is killed in the process."

Leonard Lyons visits me occasionally, and if possible I give him wisecracks for his column. "The toughest role in the world," I say to him, "is that of someone with a reputation as a wit. I make one good crack every five years. The rest of the time people sit around waiting for me to erupt."

Leonard started out in law and came to know the secret of every human heart. I gave him some of his first copy when he started his column in 1934.

In those days in New York, the press agents along Broadway would pin lousy jokes on me in order to get the name of their restaurant, or whatever they were plugging, in the paper. Walter Winchell was no exception. One night I saw him at his table in the Stork Club and said: "Don't ever print anything about me again." From then on, I was out of his column; it ended whatever friendship we had. I might mention that Winchell's favorite expression, if anyone complained about an inaccuracy in his column, was to shrug indifferently and say, "So I'm a shit-heel!" Winchell was then the most powerful influence in this country; his power was almost that of a second Federal government. But now, as Ira wrote for Jerome Kern, that is "long ago and far away." Winchell told me once: "I've just had access to my obituary notice for the New York *Times,* and let me tell you, it's terrific!" I suppose they may have revised it since.

In her early years Dorothy Parker's reputation as a wit caused her to be falsely credited with every wisecrack that made the rounds.

"Why it got so bad," she said resentfully, "that people began to laugh before I opened my mouth!"

But Dorothy Parker was an original, as a wit, a person, and a critic. She was a tiny woman, fragile and helpless, with a wispy will of iron. She loved dogs, little children, President Kennedy, and lots and lots of liquor. Even her enemies were kind to her; she brought out the maternal in everyone. At her cruelest, her voice was most caressive—the inconstant nymph. She was one of my favorite people.

I found it hard to believe that she had never gotten over her early days at the *New Yorker.* She had an Electra complex about them. She always referred to Robert Benchley and Robert Sherwood as "Mr. Benchley" and "Mr. Sherwood" when she reminisced—and she spoke of them with complete devotion.

Most of her early quips are too well known to bear repeating—but we all have our favorites. One came about when she was the book critic for the *New Yorker*. She was being pressured for her overdue copy and blithely sent word: "Too fucking busy and vice versa."

It was always hard for her to appreciate the wit of someone else. She never liked George S. Kaufman, for example. "Whoever claimed that he ever said anything funny?" she asked. It was a customary Dorothy Parker remark. About Alexander Woollcott, another critic who was not without verbal felicity, she said: "I don't see how you can like a man who said reading Proust was like bathing in someone else's dirty water." Personally, I think Woollcott made a pretty funny observation, even though I don't agree with his opinion. His description of Dorothy Parker was most perceptive. "She is," he said, " a combination of Little Eva and Lady Macbeth."

Dorothy could dig the deepest of anyone with a pen when she wanted to, however. Long ago she wrote about one of A. A. Milne's books that she "frowed up" when she read it. Milne said that it was a remark which was very hard for him to forget.

Dottie had never been able to understand the technique of psychoanalysts. She went to one once and opened up the conversation by saying, "I hated my father." That was all she could think of to say. She told me that she had no idea how other patients filled up the rest of the time. I couldn't help her on that one—it was never a problem for me.

Psychoanalysis is not for a laconic person. Dottie was usually quite taciturn, what I call a "spare speaker." The use of the exact and appropriate words—and nothing else—was always her great talent. But she was completely dependent on others for the basic necessities. She never learned how to boil water for instance, or even how to turn off a TV set.

She always retained her deceptively innocent look and her soft gentle manner. A few of her remarks I remember:

About the socialite novelist Alice Duer Miller, a beautiful woman: "How can you like a statue?"

To an upset friend who had to get rid of a cat: "Have you tried curiosity?"

To my wife: "I say this behind your back—you don't have a pore in your face."

As a game, a movie director once handed out some pornographic pictures to his writer friends for captions. Below the picture of an indescribably entwined couple, Dorothy wrote: "Good friends."

One Halloween, she was watching some of the guests ducking for apples. "There, but for a typographical error, is the story of my life," she said.

A clue to her own taste was that she liked the writing of Abraham Lincoln the best and that of Clare Boothe Luce the least.

She was told that Claire Luce was kind to her inferiors.

"But where does she find them?" she asked.

She was a nut on real-life crimes. One of her favorites was the Judd-Snyder murder case some forty-odd years ago. She told me that when Judd was in hiding, he took a cab from Manhattan to Long Island—quite a long trip—and then, she said, "not to attract attention, he gave the driver a ten-cent tip."

In her later years she was taken to a sanitarium. She told her doctor: "This is a nice room in a very nice place, but you know I have to go out for an hour or so every day to get a drink." The doctor told her solemnly that if she did not stop drinking she would be dead in a month. She smiled and sighed. "Promises, promises!" she said softly.

It seemed to me she had a great will to self-destruction. She taught some classes at a California state college. The last week of the semester, she gave an interview to the Los Angeles *Times* in which she was quoted as saying that she had never endured such stupid people. The next day, when she entered the classroom, members of the class had written out her old Communist record on the blackboard. The irony was that she had enjoyed teaching and had been fond of many of the students.

On a New Year's Eve, a few of us attended an enormous Hollywood party. We had scarcely inched our way in the door when Dorothy was swept out of sight by hordes of milling celebrants. Her husband, Alan Campbell, and friend Gene Solow went looking for her in alarm. They returned sometime later, chuckling and holding their sides in glee. They had found her, seated contentedly by the side of one of the most famous stars of the screen. Her big brown eyes were fixed on him adoringly; she hung on his every word. The fact that this was the same man who had been the object of her private ridicule didn't seem to matter then.

Much later she went with a young man to the hilarious play called *Luv*. After the first five minutes she turned to him and said accusingly: "I have a feeling that you're going to *like* this." They got up and left.

I asked Alan Campbell whether Dottie ever had a twinge of guilt about her more scathing remarks. This was of particular interest to me, as I certainly have my share. Alan revealed that she never did.

When Alan died a few years ago, Dorothy's big refuge was alcohol—which is fine. I am all for any kind of refuge. Among the friends who visited her on the night her husband died, my wife asked: "Is there anything I can do for you?"

"Yes," she said. "Get me a new husband." Her unrestrained candor may have been shocking, but I sometimes wonder if it does not reflect the view of most wives. One of the finest tributes was paid to her as a poet, by Somerset Maugham: "Like Heine, she made little songs out of her great sorrows."

In 1966, for Roddy McDowall's book *Double Exposure*, Dorothy Parker wrote a commentary about me; one line read:

"He has no meanness; and it is doubtful if he ever for a moment considered murder."

And she said it behind my back.

Verbal humor, it seems to me, is like a flash of lightning. But I know that most writers put it together laboriously and lovingly. George S. Kaufman used to idolize the writings of Mark Twain, who worked this way. Robert Benchley did it the same way. And so does S. J. Perelman.

A few years ago I was interested to read in the London *Observer* an exchange of open letters where a paraphrase of mine was mistakenly credited to Sid Perelman. The remark was "Imitation is the sincerest form of plagiarism." The next time I saw Sid, who naturally had no knowledge of it, we agreed that it was impossible to protect one's own wisecracks. I finally concluded: It doesn't matter who says it first, it's who gets credit for it last that counts.

About a year ago, Kenneth Tynan also interviewed Groucho Marx and S. J. Perelman for the London *Observer*. I was flattered to be selected by them as one of the three fastest men on the draw for one-line impromptus—the other two were George S. Kaufman and screenwriter Irving Brecher.

Perelman and Brecher worked on some of the Marx Brothers' pictures—as did many writers, at different times.

When the Marxes began in movies they missed the "feel" of a live audience that they had in musical comedies like *Cocoanuts*. One of their best pictures was *A Night at the Opera*. It started out as one of the worst. George Kaufman was one of the writers as well as the supervisor of the film, along with Irving Thalberg, the reigning MGM genius; the director, Sam Wood, later became famous when he served in the same capacity on the tearjerker *Goodbye, Mr. Chips,* but with the Marxes he was chosen because he was flexible and would let the brothers cavort as they wanted to on the screen.

When the picture was finished, Kaufman took it to a theater for a preview. It was a disaster. There was hardly a laugh in the audience. It was rushed indignantly to another theater. The audience reaction was almost exactly the same. So they took it back to the studio to ponder upon the phenomenon.

It was Kaufman who came up with the solution. What had been missing was the uncanny timing of the Marx Brothers on the stage. But this factor could be largely controlled by a pair of scissors. Kaufman and Thalberg spent days in going over the film again and again, snipping out perhaps nine minutes of a movie that lasted two hours. The result was a smash comedy success.

The Marx Brothers were always a closely knit group—but they also understood their relative values as performers. When they were working on Broadway, Zeppo, the "straight" man and consequently replaceable, decided to quit the show. Sam Harris, the producer, gave him permission to leave. When Groucho, Harpo, and Chico heard about it, they went to Harris. Groucho said: "Sam, you'll have to give us more money if Zeppo leaves."

Incidentally, Groucho told me that when he became sick in Chicago, Zeppo took his place and was terrific in the part.

Sam Harris, once the top producer of Broadway (and incidentally the manager of Terry McGovern, the fighter, at one time), was beloved by all. He was one of the friendliest and most appreciative—and most successful—entrepreneurs in the theater. On a certain occasion he was visiting a friend who became deathly ill. Sam, terribly affected, rushed down to the telephone on the first floor and phoned for an emergency ambulance. He completed the call and fainted on the spot. The ambulance rushed over. It picked Harris up and took him to the hospital instead of his friend.

In 1958, when I had my TV show, I received a letter from Gummo Marx, the lesser-known brother who was one of the original members of the act until he decided to become a businessman. He wrote:

"I heard you use the word 'Euphoria' on your show. I haven't heard this used since I was a child, when my mother used to say to us, 'Go out and play.' We would ask 'Who?' And she would reply, 'Euphoria.' "

When Sir Cedric Hardwicke appeared on my show, he said that George Bernard Shaw had told him that he was his fifth favorite actor—the other four were the Marx Brothers.

Sir Cedric also told a story involving the funeral of an old-time English performer named George Robey, who was famous in the London music halls of the time. It was said that W. C. Fields bought many of his routines.

When Robey died, all of show business turned out. Among the mourners at the cemetery was a doddering old fellow. He was asked by a friend how old he was.

"Ninety-five," quavered the mourner.

"Ah," said the friend, "it's hardly worth the trouble of going home, is it?"

Then there is the story that Eddie Cantor told about Bert Williams, the colored star of the Ziegfeld Follies who became famous long before there was any civil rights sympathy. In the days when prejudice ran rampant, Bert stopped in at a swank bar and ordered a shot of whiskey.

"That'll cost you fifty dollars," the bartender said curtly.

Bert dug into his pocket and spread $250 on the bar. "Give me five," he said quietly.

Chico Marx, the "Italian" brother, was a compulsive gambler. Some of the best Marx Brothers pictures were made simply to give him the cash to get out of debt. He was the oldest and also the favorite of Minnie, the mother Marx. (Groucho was number three in her affection, which perhaps accounts for his abrasive disposition.)

New York show people were the first to discover Sigmund

Freud, but Zeppo Marx was one of the first in Hollywood to begin dating a psychiatrist.

Some of Zeppo's troubles probably stemmed from the fact that he was the best street fighter I ever saw. He really liked a rough-and-tumble. But this talent also got him started as a Hollywood agent. He was in a Santa Monica amusement park, and some churl commenced to annoy his friend, the successful writer Norman Krasna. Zeppo turned on him and knocked out the heckler with one punch.

"From this minute on," cried Krasna, slapping him on the back, "you're my agent!"

I saw Zeppo not long ago. "Had any fistfights lately?" I asked him.

"Had one about a month ago," he sighed. "It was very tough." Then, for the first time, I knew Zeppo was getting old.

It was one of the brothers who announced despairingly one night: "I can lay anyone in the world but my wife!" I thought then and think now that it was not only a good line but also a vastly accurate philosophic observation on most marriages.

When I did the *Kraft Music Hall* radio show with Al Jolson in the late forties, we went to New York each year for two weeks. Groucho was a guest on one of those trips; consequently the three of us spent a great deal of time together. Whenever we were in a public spot, restaurant, or elevator, or just walking along, people would stop and ask Jolson and me for our autographs. Nobody recognized Groucho, and for a very good reason.

Up until then, Groucho's moustache had only been a prop. I mean it was painted on for his stage and movie roles. After his experience with us, he grew his own moustache, and it has remained there permanently for every occasion.

Groucho and screenwriter-director Nunnally Johnson are very close. They like each other's humor and each other's company. They even have certain signals to communicate their feelings during a dinner party. On one occasion, Groucho was amazed to see Nunnally get up and leave without even giving him an SOS. He caught up to his friend later that evening and asked him the reason.

"Because of what the hostess said to me," said Nunnally.

"What did she say?"

"She pointed to Sid Luft and said: 'That's the most interesting man in Hollywood.' "

"All you could do was leave," Groucho agreed.

Nunnally is one of my favorite wits. He told me that one of his children never spoke a word from birth until he was two years old. Then one day out in the backyard an airplane went over. The child, according to Nunnally, pointed upward and said distinctly: "That's a *DC-6*." Nunnally says he is raising one of his brood to play baseball so that by the time the boy is ready to become a professional he can be outstanding—the only white player in the big leagues.

Harpo Marx was always adored by all intellectuals, but for what reason I could never discover. Except, of course, that he was uniquely lovable. He even made a great conquest of friendship when he met George Bernard Shaw in the late twenties. Years ago, I asked George Kaufman if he had heard from Harpo. "How?" he asked. "How can you hear from Harpo? He can't write, and he can't talk, so how can you hear from Harpo?"

In his later years Harpo made his home near Palm Springs. When I had my Los Angeles television show in 1958, I did hear from Harpo.

EL RANCHO HARPO

Dear Os. Some years ago. I was hear in California and you were in N.Y. and you met George Kaufman you asked him if he ever heres from Harpo and he answered how tis true i seldom write in fact this is the first leter in about ten years the last one was to George B. Shaw he never answerd me so i figured whats the use of writing he gave me a fist addation of St. Joan i seldom can get chanel 13 if you ever have a fight if you ever have a fight i like that line change two to four or five

my best to June

Harpo

Because of the mountains, it was difficult for him to get Channel 13 (my station) at his home. One night, a few months after his letter, he walked in unexpectedly while my show was on the air. Naturally, I was delighted to see him and persuaded him to appear on camera. He did—but in true Harpo style he didn't say a word.

Once in New York my daughter attended a small dinner party. Among the guests were Harpo and his wife Susan. Later my daughter was asked by Jonathan Miller the English wit for details of the evening, what goodies were bandied about, what Harpo said, etc.

"He didn't say anything," she reported.

"How about his wife?" he asked eagerly.

"She didn't say anything, either."

"Oh," he sniffed in mock disgust. "Stealing Harpo's bit, eh?"

Harpo liked to tell stories of when I first arrived on the West Coast. It was he who determined to give me my first vision of the Pacific Ocean. He said it was the greatest sight in the business. I couldn't have cared less, but he finally got me into a car and away we went to the beach.

In those days, it was completely uncluttered by beach houses, boardwalks, hot dog stands, or human beings. It was just there: stark stretches of clean gray sand and blue water as far as you could see.

"There," said Harpo happily. "How do you like it?"

"Hey," I said, "a Gentile ocean!"

Harpo and I used to compete for the beautiful girls that kept pouring into Hollywood from all over the country. I recall that

Harpo was visited by one of his many female fanciers unexpectedly—only to find him in the nude, playing his harp.

But Harpo could be topped. Once, when the trains were still carrying passengers, Harpo came down to the Pasadena station to see a friend off for the East. He saw two old ladies seated in the dining car. On impulse, he rushed onto the train, seized the menu, and tore it up and devoured it.

Unperturbed, one lady turned to the headwaiter. "Please let us have another menu," she said. "Someone has eaten ours."

The Marxes are sometimes funnier as individuals than they were as a professional team. Anyone is taken as fair game for a gag. At one party which Groucho attended with his wife, Eden, she told everyone that she was taking some courses at UCLA.

"What courses?" I inquired. "Courses in what?"

"Perversion," Groucho snapped before she could reply.

Groucho also told a joke about Adam and Eve that was unusually clean for him. It ran like this: Adam proposed marriage to Eve. She gave him no answer, and Adam said suspiciously: "Is there another man?" Of course, I remarked, Adam could have said: "Is this another rib?"

At a memorial service honoring the late poet T. S. Eliot, the speakers were Kenneth Tynan, Laurence Olivier, and Groucho Marx. Afterward I told Groucho that Eliot was a violent anti-Semite. I had been told that he would go into a room, look around—and if there were any Jews present, he would wait five minutes and then discreetly leave.

"What the hell," Groucho replied, "I don't like a lot of Jews, either."

Many of the former literary lights owed their discovery to Franklin P. Adams, the columnist who was known as FPA. Probably the outstanding protégé of FPA was George S. Kaufman. Dorothy Parker also gave Frank Adams credit for helping her perfect her writing style.

I've always been a baby, but this is how it started.

Left to right: with my three older brothers, Harry, Howard, seated Ben, me, and standing behind me, my uncle, Dr. Maurice Radin.

Pittsburgh, Pa., Jan. 3, 19

My Dear Dear mamma:

I past to room 9 n the second floor. I am glad that you went to New York, but when you will come back home I w be more glad, so will be papa and Hony and every body will be glad to ha you home. I am not cry and not fighting with so but I would rather have home

good by my dear mamma. Your loving son Oscar

Written at the age of seven.

My mother.

Down in front left: me next to my brother Howard. *In back row center:* brother Bennie.

I was about seventeen in this one.

In *Burlesque,* a play produced by Arthur Hopkins, I played the part of a songwriter. Seated at the piano, with *(left to right)* Eileen Wilson, Charles D. Brown, Barbara Stanwyck, and Hal Skelly.

Picture of Arnold Schoenberg, inscribed.

Caricature of me by George Gershwin.

Oscar by George
Mar 27 '3

On the occasion of a concert at the Lewisohn Stadium in New York, 1931. *Left to right:* me, viola player Otto Langley, composer George Gershwin, Robert Russell Bennett, conductor Fritz Reiner, composer Deems Taylor, and conductor William Merigan Daly.

1939. Radio show *Information Please*. Me, John Kieran, Dorothy Parker, F.P.A.

Recital for Paderewski. I am second from left, last row. *Seated center:* Paderewski and my piano teacher, Sigismund Stojowski.

George Gershwin took this picture of me around 1936.
In the background the picture is "Dr. Devaraigne," by Modigliani—one in the collection of Impressionist paintings that George acquired in the early '30s.

I accompanied Jack Benny when he made his "concert debut" at Carnegie Hall for a charity performance.

Westport, Connecticut. With Alfred Vanderbilt, our house guest.

Forbes Field in Pittsburgh. War Bond Show during World War II. *Back row:* Pvt. John Payne (actor), actor Paul Lukas, Paul Whiteman, Lt. William Holden (when he was in the Army Air Force). *Front row:* I am seated next to Ingrid Bergman, and Ray Bolger is next.

Early radio show with Frank Sinatra.

With Erich Leinsdorf when I played with him and the Cleveland Symphony. Leinsdorf is at present the conductor of the Boston Symphony.

With Harpo Marx at the home of the George S. Kaufmans in Bucks County, Pennsylvania.

Warner Bros. Studios. On the set of the movie *The Corn Is Green* with Bette Davis. Talking to Irving Rapper and Miss Davis.

A Smattering of Ignorance, my first book, was published in 1940. I couldn't put it down.

Herbert Bayard Swope and I acting as bartenders at a charity ball.

With Eugene Ormandy, conductor of the Philadelphia Philharmonic Orchestra.

George S. Kaufman and I cohosted and wrote a radio show for six weeks in 1943.

The Barkleys of Broadway, movie with Ginger Rogers.

For two years—1947 and 1948—I was on the *Kraft Music Hall* radio show with the great Al Jolson. Here we are with Lucille Ball when she was a guest. *(Kraft Foods Photo)*

I received this photograph from President Truman shortly after I had played a recital at the White House on the occasion of a state dinner for the Supreme Court.

A scene from *Humoresque*, with John Garfield and Joan Crawford.

A scene with Doris Day from her first picture, *Romance on the High Seas*.

The movie *Rhythm on the River,* with Bing Crosby and Mary Martin.

After I played with Toscanini, he inscribed this picture to June.

Seated between Jack Warner and director Mervyn Le Roy.

Warner Bros. Studios, 1944. On the set of *A Rhapsody in Blue.* Me, producer Jesse Lasky, Ira and Leonore Gershwin, Robert Alda.

As soloist with Paul Whiteman and orchestra for *A Rhapsody in Blue*.

Talking to Igor Stravinsky, who came to visit.

1941. *Information Please. Left to right:* John Kieran, F.P.A., Wendell Wilkie, and me.

With Judy Garland.

Vladimir Horowitz.

After my marriage to June.

Our first daughter, Marcia.

Liza Minnelli and Amanda.

June and the children—Amanda, four; Lorna, seven; Marcia, nine, as they visited the set of *An American in Paris*.

Information Please traveled to California. *Left to right:* Mrs. F. P. Adams, Clifton Fadiman, Mrs. Dan Golenpaul, Mrs. Fadiman with her arm around Jonathan Fadiman, Joe Bell, NBC producer, June holding our second daughter, Lorna, me holding Marcia. *Seated:* Dan Golenpaul, F.P.A., John Kieran.

On the set of the movie *The Barkleys of Broadway*. Amanda, three; Lorna, six; Marcia, 8.

Arriving in California from New York to do a movie. June holding our third daughter, Amanda. *Down front:* Lorna and Marcia, looking pretty glum—that was the day they came down with the mumps.

With June—Lorna, Amanda, Marcia, at home, Beverly Hills.

Sammy Davis, Jr., was on my show three times.

Also Steve Allen.

And Leo Durocher.

On my Los Angeles TV show in 1958.
June read questions sent in by the viewers.

Aldous Huxley was also a guest on my
local TV show in 1958.

Jerry Lewis gagged it up.

I was working pretty hard in those days. So I took a quick nap on camera once in a
while.

Justice William O. Douglas came on my show.

Christopher Isherwood appeared with me many times.

With Adlai Stevenson at M.G.M. Studio. 1956.

Premiere of *An American in Paris.* Mr. and Mrs. Arthur Freed (producer), Leslie Caron, George Hormel, to whom she was then married, June and I.

Seen in action as I played George Gershwin's Concerto in F for *An American in Paris.*

Fred Allen and I did a movie together. This is a scene from *O. Henry's Full House.*

With Fred Astaire, rehearsing for my L.A. TV show.

1951. With Gene Kelly during the film-
ing of *An American in Paris*.

I got tired of sitting at the piano, so I
showed him a step or two.

LA625 0B021   1958 JUN 21 20 PM 9 11

O PNA688 PD=TDPN SAN MARINO CALIF 20 840PMP=

:OSCAR LEVANT=

　　　　　STATION KCOP LOSA=

HAVE JUST CANCELLED ORDER FOR MY 15TH PHILCO I DON'T

NEED ANYBODY EITHER BUT YOU ARE A GOOD DEED IN A NAUGHTY

　WORLD MAZURAKA PLEASE=

　　　　　FRANK LLOYD WRIGHT=

Received this telegram during a public controversy with a sponsor
on my TV show. Subsequently everything was settled, although I
was off the air for a few days.

At a social event June talked to Groucho
Marx as Clifton Fadiman listened.

And I sat between Mr. and Mrs. Eric
Ambler (Joan Harrison).

June reading my *Memoirs.*

When I appeared on a Jack Paar Show. *(NBC-TV Press Photo)*

By the time I met him on *Information Please,* Frank had five children and was getting on in years. But he was still witty and droll. It was he who said: "The average American is above average."

He also once said to George Kaufman's wife, Beatrice, "Guess whose birthday it is?"

"Yours?" asked Beatrice.

"No," said Frank, "but you're getting warm. It's Shakespeare's!"

George Kaufman was the most talented all-around craftsman I ever knew as a writer, wit, critic, and director. For a period of time he was very much underrated and, in some cases, forgotten—but in the past two years several of his plays have been successfully revived. He was the man whose dry, funny, understated style gave a whole new flavor and direction to the stage. He squeezed the flamboyant nonsense out of it.

Kaufman started out as a newspaperman. One afternoon in the twenties in the New York *Times* office of Alexander Woollcott were gathered George Kaufman, editor of the same paper's entertainment page, and Marc Connelly, the drama critic of the New York *Telegraph.*

The repartee was good enough to be put on any stage. Finally the idea germinated between Kaufman and Connelly that destiny had selected them to write plays together. "Why don't we try it?" asked Connelly. They wrote five straight hits in collaboration. During those years they each took time out to write a play alone. George then collaborated with other writers, notably Edna Ferber and Moss Hart. He was also invaluable as a "play doctor" for other playwrights. When one of his own shows developed problems on the road, he said ironically, "What this play needs is George S. Kaufman."

To mention a few of his achievements in directing, it was he who directed that fine newspaper play, *The Front Page,* by Hecht and MacArthur, and who saved the musical *Guys and*

Dolls by his adroit stage knowledge. On the other hand, he had a near miss with *The American Way*. I did the music and conducted for that show; I remember there were about four hundred people in the cast with Fredric March. The reviews were not good, but Kaufman said: "They are just." Kaufman also directed John Steinbeck's *Of Mice and Men* and took on plays like *The Late George Apley*. They were all resounding successes, but Kaufman really preferred comedies such as *The Man Who Came to Dinner*. He was psychologically bruised about Steinbeck. Steinbeck was frightened of New York at first sight and crept in and out of alleys while he was there. Even after the play was a big hit, he never saw or phoned Kaufman again.

George was tall, dour, and solemn with the slightly forbidding look of a startled egghead. Not everyone was comfortable in his presence. He not only discouraged any outward display of intimacy or sentimentality; he literally dreaded the back-slappers and the hand-pumpers. After he had suffered through a phony potboiler drama by Sam Shipman in which a character ostentatiously referred to his great wealth, George satirized it in one line. "Tell my fifteen-piece orchestra to strike up a tune," he would command the butler with a blasé wave of his hand.

His puns were incessant, and one in particular incorporated the names of two well-known women of the twenties: "Agna Enters where Peggy Fears to tread."

(Puns are the lowest form of wit—if you don't happen to think of them first.)

Kaufman's favorite tune was from Noel Coward's *Private Lives,* "Someday I'll Find You." George would paraphrase the lyrics to "Someday I'll Find You, Creep up Behind You."

Somebody said ecstatically to George that he had seen a certain play three times. "What's the matter?" Kaufman asked lightly. "Didn't you get it the first time?"

On another occasion Kaufman was being high-pressured by

a gold mine salesman who informed him that the mine was so productive he could pick up pieces of gold from the ground. "You mean I have to bend over?" inquired George dryly.

Kaufman was a guest one evening at the home of the Charlie MacArthurs. Mrs. MacArthur, Helen Hayes, had a shy manner of speaking, frequently garbling her words. At a point in the evening she hospitably announced: "Anybody who wants my piano is willing to it."

George looked up from the bridge table. "Helen, that's very seldom of you," he responded in kind.

As a director George was always soft-spoken and considerate of actors. During the run of a play he would, at intervals, stop by the theater to make sure that all was running smoothly. On one of these occasions he was horrified to discover the liberties that William Gaxton had taken with his performance in *Of Thee I Sing*. At intermission George went out and sent a telegram to Gaxton: "Am sitting in the last row. Wish you were here."

Gaxton was always very fond of himself in his roles, and sometimes this unconsciously worked into his conversation. He heard that the father of Richard Rodgers had died. Gaxton sought him out and said with transparent sincerity: "I'm sorry to hear your father died, Dick. He always liked me." Dick had only lost a father; Gaxton had lost a fan.

Kaufman only directed one movie, but he was much impressed by the direction of Orson Welles in *The Magnificent Ambersons,* a Tarkington book translated to the screen.

The only movie that Kaufman directed he wrote with Nunnally Johnson. It was called *The Senator Was Indiscreet,* with William Powell in the leading role. Although the picture received scanty approval (Westbrook Pegler denounced it as un-American), I found much of it hilarious. It was then considered a cartoon—a pompous windbag Senator, crooked politicians, and a final burlesque sequence on the credibility of election oratory. By today's standards it doesn't seem too inaccurate.

There were a few high spots:

"Senator, what is your stand on inflation?"

"I'm against it."

"How about deflation?"

"I'm against it."

"What are you for?"

"Flation!"

The final scene had the Senator at a Madison Square Garden rally, making an election eve speech:

"And for all those *not* in the armed services, two thousand dollars a year," he thundered.

At a dinner party that Groucho once gave at a restaurant in Hollywood there were many friends from the old days. I suggested that we wire George Kaufman in New York to tell him that we were sorry that he wasn't with us. George's response was typical.

"Couldn't think of a worse place to be," he wired back.

In his declining years, after a long siege of illness, Kaufman had an accidental encounter with a distinguished lady author whom he hadn't seen in ages. "Why, Peggy!" he exclaimed in tired surprise. Then he stared at her sadly. "I thought we were both dead," he said.

Kaufman's great skill—as I guess it must be in any great director—was objective assessment. He would estimate his own talents, those of others, and the worth of a script very accurately. Joe Mankiewicz, the Hollywood writer-director, was always saying that he would do a play on Broadway. "I want to live long enough to see a Mankiewicz play on Broadway," Kaufman said skeptically. Although he did live to a fairly ripe age, he didn't live that long.

The team of Kaufman and Hart, as everyone knows, was highly successful. They were not as fortunate in one of their early collaborations. *Merrily We Roll Along,* directed by George, was the first serious effort of Moss Hart. Kaufman wanted me to play the part of a piano player in the party scene for *Merrily.* I half agreed, then got the script. I glanced at it and was overwhelmed with terror. I threw it in his face and ran out.

The play itself concerned a successful playwright of fluffy comedies, who had a palatial home on Long Island, where he gave glittering parties attended by famous celebrities. (Kaufman and Hart used prototypes of the celebrities of the day— Dorothy Parker making jokes, George Gershwin playing the piano, etc.) Yet the playwright in the play was very miserable— and why? Because he had really wanted to be a serious dramatist and write about coal miners and their problems.

As the writer Herman Mankiewicz (Joe's brother) said, "What a terrible plight."

It was a big flop.

Moss Hart acquired an imposing summer home in Bucks County, Pennsylvania, where the most important member of the household seemed to be his butler, Charles. One evening as cocktails were being served, Charles interrupted the conversation and dramatically announced that the sunset must be viewed. There was a polite murmur, and a few guests drifted toward the windows, but Charles was adamant in his insistence that we *all* partake of this visual delight. What the hell, I thought with irritation, a lousy sunset is no match for good conversation.

The trees on the property also received their share of attention. They had been transplanted at great expense, an undertaking that inspired S. N. Behrman's remark: "It only shows what God could do if he had money."

Moss was completely engaging, gregarious, witty, and kind. As he progressed in his career his judgment, stagewise, was usually infallible. He became a brilliant director with such gems as *My Fair Lady* and *Camelot* to his credit.

Despite my reputation for surliness, I was usually the one that my friends confided in when they came to the crossroads of their careers. In the early days, Moss took me for a long aside to tell me his decision that he had to fly out of George Kaufman's nest and work alone. I encouraged him. He did very well —and got back some of the money he was spending on psychoanalysis—with his *Lady in the Dark*. But Moss was largely predictable in his desire to go on his own in his personal life. I made one of my more bruited-about remarks at a dinner party where Moss came in accompanying the stately and beautiful actress Edith Atwater.

"Ah," I said, "here comes Moss Hart and the future Miss Atwater."

Moss persevered in his analysis, however, with excellent results. He eventually married lovely Kitty Carlisle and had a very happy marriage. It was Kaufman who observed wryly long afterward, "What a twist! Here I am, going to an analyst, and Moss has two kids."

Alexander Woollcott, in his early days as a theater critic, was not only exasperating to his victims; he also incurred the animosity of his own colleagues. George Jean Nathan in a deprecating article described him as "The Seidlitz Powder in Times Square." (The Bromo-Seltzer of its time.) Woollcott was obviously the bubbly, effervescent, giddy new high priest of Broadway. Nathan went on to say: "His appraisals of his feminine favorites read like a bewitched college boy writing and beseeching a lock of hair."

The Woollcott style variated between great bursts of admiration and opprobrious condemnations—"The actor should have been gently but firmly shot at sunrise," for example.

A compulsive talker, Woollcott could not tolerate loquacity in others. His long friendship with Noel Coward finally wore itself out when neither one could bear to go on listening to the other. Woollcott also complained to his friends about me: "Talking to Oscar is like fighting a man who has three fists instead of the regulation two," he said.

Woollcott and Coward used to play the popular game of the day, backgammon, quite a lot. Their conversation was irritatingly amiable; shafts of wit would be interchanged. Noel would say, "Alex, I suspect you of being shifty." Woollcott paraphrased Noel's dialogue from *Private Lives* when he replied, "There isn't a particle of you that I know, remember, or want."

It was a unique era that Woollcott belonged to, and of which he was so much a part. He was the tyrant, benevolent or otherwise, of a large group of extraordinarily successful people. The so-called intelligentsia banded together in their perusal of fun, feuds, and fame. Dorothy Parker dubbed Woollcott's apartment Wit's End. Woollcott likened Harold Ross, the editor of the *New Yorker,* to a "dishonest Abe Lincoln." Edna Ferber snipped about Woollcott: "This New Jersey Nero who mistakes his pinafore for a toga." But Edna Ferber was often blunt. When she said to me, "Oscar, I never thought you'd amount to much," for once in my life, I was speechless.

Woollcott, of course, had a genius for being offensive. Ludwig Lewisohn complained about getting a bad review. He was instantly squelched. "Ludwig thinks he gets bad reviews because the critics are anti-Semitic," said Woollcott. "Actually, it's because Ludwig has halitosis."

Woollcott's favorite play, he said, was the great English version of World War I, R. C. Sherriff's *Journey's End.* (Dorothy Parker hated this kind of sentimentality that had to do with Alice in Wonderland and war.) As I recall, it used some realism in profanity—but in this it was behind Shaw. I believe the first such expression on the stage in England was his "bloody," used in *Pygmalion* in 1913. In those days it was considerable of a shocker, when ladies used to faint and gentlemen walk out at a single "damn." In this country, the first profanity was post-World War I, in *What Price Glory?* by Laurence Stallings. Woollcott had read the original manuscript and brought it to the attention of producer Arthur Hopkins. Until Stallings did some additional excellent work, he was always embarrassed when anyone mentioned he had written it. "I don't want to be known as a one-play writer," he said.

It was Woollcott who was the first to cry up the fine talent of Evelyn Waugh in this country. Waugh himself occasionally gave a point to the critics. In one of his best books, *A Handful of Dust,* he had the hero imprisoned for life in the South American jungle while being forced to read Charles Dickens to a half-mad planter. He got complaints from his readers and actually published an alternate ending in which the fellow returned triumphant to his English estates.

With Harpo Marx and writer Charlie Lederer, I once reluctantly agreed to visit Lake Bomoseen, the island resort in Vermont that belonged to Woollcott and his friends. It was a great place for everyone to play games, I was told, everything from croquet to bridge. But I never could stand the wide open spaces —and the only game I knew how to play was checkers. However, I went.

On our arrival actress Margalo Gillmore was busy reciting a new poem by Rudyard Kipling, his first (and last, as it turned out) poem in years.

I suddenly got such a severe pain in my Achilles' tendon that I literally could not walk. A doctor was called in, he taped it up, and I went back to New York that same afternoon. It was probably the shortest visit ever paid to Woollcott's island.

What Woollcott did not know was that in those days I did everything with an overwhelming sense of inadequacy. I was using up three personalities and had no psychic cushion to fall back on. Anyway, that was my first (but not last) experience with a psychogenic pain.

Harpo and Charlie and I were also together the night that we turned on the radio to listen to Woollcott on a political panel show.

After the opening statements, there was a period of ten minutes when Woollcott's voice was not heard. Harpo, who loved Woollcott and who knew that he had not been in good health, became worried. When we heard the ambulance siren, we suspected the worst. That was the night that Woollcott died.

Whatever you thought of Woollcott, he had guts—literally and figuratively. He got bored with being a critic and gave it up cold. He got bored with his radio show and gave it up the same way. The one thing he loved to do was act.

He played in a road company of *The Man Who Came to Dinner,* the part that was written about him by Kaufman and Hart. The following letter * was written to Charlie Lederer from San Francisco. Woollcott was there with the show and I had just given a concert.

San Francisco, Calif.
March 26, 1940

Dear Bosie:

Oscar [Levant] came and went like a tornado, accompanied by his pregnant bride, and staying here at the Fairmont because I had suggested it. As it is extremely expensive he grew more bitter with every check he had to sign. My major triumph was seeing to it that his telephone call to Harpo, which he made from my room, was charged to his. At the concert his performance was truly incandescent. After he had finished the "Rhapsody," Claudia Morgan and I joined him backstage and through the peephole we watched Monteux conduct the final Sibelius and Ravel

---

* From *The Letters of Alexander Woollcott,* Vol. II, ed. by Beatrice Kaufman and Joseph Hennessey. Copyright 1944 by The Viking Press, Inc. Reprinted by permission of The Viking Press, Inc.

numbers. With the concert finally over Oscar and I, heading for the green room, debouched into the corridor where a comely Miss with an autograph book was lying in wait. "Oh! Mr. Woollcott," she said, "may I have your autograph?" With a bellow of pain, Oscar left for New York.

A.W.

Chapter 5

$\mathcal{W}$HEN my wife and I went to see the new movie star—Julie Christie—we were very much impressed. June said she was every inch a princess. I was reminded of the old crack of somebody being "every other inch a queen," but I kept quiet. Then June said: "Just like Grace Kelly." That did it.

"Grace Kelly," I said, "is every inch a Kelly. What's more," I added, "she just married the first prince who asked her."

The recent visit of Princess Grace to the scene of her former movie triumphs brought forth an amazed reaction to the changes she found in the movie industry. "I'll never get over Universal Studios," she was quoted as saying. "They're so horribly commercial, so crowded with sightseers. Where's the personal touch? It's vanished. I couldn't work under such conditions."

Second to Disneyland, the biggest tourist attraction in Southern California is now Universal City. The last bit of evidence I shall offer in this respect is the following story. Lew Wasserman, once the head of the octopoidal agency, the Music Corporation of America, and now head of Universal Studios, recently took Howard Koch of Paramount for a tour of his new domain. He showed him the city, the bank, the brokerage office, the sets, the tourists, the bus caravans, the TV studios, and all there was to show. Except for one thing.

"What about motion pictures?" Koch inquired.

"Oh, that!" Lew said indifferently. "That's only seven percent of our product."

Probably one of the things that contributed most to the decline of Hollywood is the lack of replacements for people like the late Humphrey Bogart. I used to go to his house occasionally. I would invariably encounter the biggest hazard there (outside Bogie himself), which consisted of two very large boxer dogs. They would sleep all evening in the middle of the living room. Naturally, this heightened the decibel level of the conversation. It also resulted in everyone lighting kitchen matches all night long in the hope that somehow the sulphur smell would dispel the smell of the damn dogs.

Bogart once said with some heat when he was working on *Sabrina* with Audrey Hepburn, "If anyone tells me that she's wistful, charming, or radiant, I'll punch him right in the nose." Evidently Bogie had a slight case of "jel."

Bogart's great hero was Leslie Howard. He worked with him on the New York stage in *The Petrified Forest*. Arthur Hopkins, the director, was instrumental in giving Bogart that chance to play the tough gangster Duke Mantee. Bogart had only been a juvenile before that. The role opened up his whole career. When the show went on tour, the cast was deeply concerned that Leslie Howard, madly in love with Merle Oberon, might defect and return to Hollywood. As it turned out, their fears proved to be groundless. After the show closed, he and Bogie went to Hollywood to do the film version. That was the beginning of Bogart's movie career and the emergence of a man destined to become a legend.

Professionally, Bogart was a fine actor. Privately, he was a drinker and a brawler. His next to last wife was Mayo Methot, an actress, as all of them were. She could also stash away the liquor; their knock-down, drag-out bouts were notorious. When they went overseas to entertain the World War II troops, their uninhibited behavior proved too much even for the fighting men.

Bogart told of a happening on their visit to one of the battle areas. In a recreation room, enshrined over the bar, was a tall highball glass filled with a terrible concoction of many different kinds of booze. A soldier's prank, it had a sign attached challenging someone to drink it. No one had taken the dare. No one had proved that foolhardy. No one, that is, until Mayo Methot, the third Mrs. Bogart, came along. When she drank it, even Bogie was aghast.

Their return home was by request.

To Bogart's credit, he always defended his wife. She is an actress, he said, and actresses must act. The fact that her professional career was over was beside—and also—the point.

Always disciplined and conscientious about his work, Bogie confined his carousing to his private life. Yet the one can unquestionably affect the other. His last wife, Betty (Lauren Bacall), was convinced that she entered his life at a critical period. She claimed that he could not have survived another six months. It was true that his behavior and his career improved. He won the Academy Award for his performance in *The African Queen*—a triumph considering his competition (the memorable performance of Marlon Brando in *A Streetcar Named Desire*).

It was Betty who made Bogart socially acceptable to the elite of Hollywood. He also became a father for the first time.

I remember a weekend that he spent with his small son. They went by train to San Francisco so the boy could meet the engineer, sleep in a berth, eat in the diner, and so forth. That item would not have tied in with Bogart's public image. And neither would the news that his wife called him Humphrey.

Lauren Bacall or Betty Bogart or Betty Bacall (now Betty Lauren Robards) always liked me. I think it was because she looks a little like me. But she was always too much for my spirit to carry. She has too much energy. She kissed me good-bye once and said she was going to New York.

"Is there anything I can do for you?" she wanted to know. She treated me with a maternal touch that could have led to trouble.

She is a wonderful girl and always great fun at a party—her breezy animation and ribald sense of humor can enliven any event. At a gala New Year's Eve party, one of the distinguished guests happened to be the Shah of Iran. He and Betty went whirling around the dance floor; a fragment of their conversation was reported as follows:

"You dance beautifully, Miss Bacall."

"You bet your ass, Shah."

Betty started out in the theatrical world as an usherette at the St. James Theater. She once did a picture with Herman Shumlin and told me a story about this rather grim and glum producer who descended from Broadway to Hollywood. He was producing some opus or other at Warner Brothers, and there arose the necessity for the sound of a pistol shot. This is usually done, of course, by dubbing in the explosion later on a sound track. But Shumlin, realistic to the end, insisted on having a real pistol fired off. They did. It proved to carry a real bullet which caromed off the private office of Harry Warner. There was hell to pay, but no one could ever prove it was an assassination attempt.

I did a movie, *Cobweb,* with Betty Bacall. It was also the first picture for John Kerr, the young New York actor who had made a big hit in the play *Tea and Sympathy.* He later did his original part in the film version, but *Cobweb* was his first screen role.

Jack Kerr was also wanted—not just wanted, *besieged*—by producer Leland Hayward and director Billy Wilder for the leading role in their production *The Spirit of St. Louis.* The role of Charles Lindbergh would have been an enormous break for any young actor, yet Jack was absolutely adamant in his refusal to play it. His reasons were, I think, twofold. The first was an actor's normal concern that too close an identification with a historical figure could prove a detriment for future roles. Secondly, and this is just an assumption, his personal beliefs may have been so alien to those of Lindbergh that he could not relish the idea of playing the man. I must say he had the character to stand by his decision.

The part was eventually played brilliantly by James Stewart. Unfortunately, he was twenty years too old for it.

Betty Bacall always formed strong attachments with co-workers she liked; she wanted them around her constantly. During *Cobweb,* Jack and I (with wives) were invited often to her home. It was the house of her dreams, the one she had chosen after she had housebroken Bogie.

Last year John Kerr played the continuing role of the district attorney in the television serial *Peyton Place.* It is therefore interesting to note that Jack, a Harvard graduate, has now in real life taken up the study of law. The quixotic procedure of TV justice may have been a persuading factor.

When I met Charles Boyer, who was also in the picture *Cobweb,* I found him very friendly and courteous, but also

reticent. I asked him about how he learned to act. He told me
that when he was young, he had made a point of seeing all the
plays in which Lucien Guitry, the great French actor, appeared.
He said he had learned from this kind of close observation. He
never saw Lucien repeat himself, even in redoing the same
scenes. "He gave some very strange readings," Boyer said, "but
he was always inventive and original, more than any other
actor I have ever seen."

Perhaps my ideas of wit are a little morbid. One of the early
French movies that I liked best was *The Story of a Cheat*. It was
written by the witty French playwright, Sacha Guitry, the son
of Lucien.

The opening scene showed a child doing something wrong
for which he was sent to bed without supper. The main dish
at the meal was mushrooms—poisonous ones, as it turned out;
consequently all of his family died painful deaths. The moral
drawn was clear—because the child had been bad he was saved.
I thought it a clever and sardonic way to open a film.

I remember a reaction to a movie of the forties—*The Song of
Bernadette*, which glorified the village of Lourdes in France.
A disgruntled critic said the whole production was "a gigantic
real estate venture blessed by the Lord."

Another reaction came from the South Pacific, where my
friend Alfred Vanderbilt was stationed during the war. He
wrote that the boys in his group were pretty upset, having
thought that *The Song of Bernadette* was going to be a musical.

I like to call the older geniuses of Hollywood the Dry-Rot
Group. But about all that is left is Darryl Zanuck. Zanuck has
always been one of a kind—with a due sense of his own im-
portance. Joe Kennedy once told me that of all the people invited to lunch at St. James during his term as ambassador to
England, the only one who was late was Darryl.

It was Zanuck who established possibly the most arbitrary method of cutting known to the motion picture industry. He was sitting in his private projection booth reviewing the rough-cut of a feature. After each reel, of course, the curtains closed and the lights went up while the projectionist threaded the next reel. Zanuck chomped his cigar and waited impatiently. After six reels, he stood up and started out. The projectionist and director shouted simultaneously: "There's another reel to come."

"The hell with it," Zanuck snorted. "That's it!" So that was it. The picture went on to be a success.

Zanuck had started his career at Warner Brothers Studio, where he had risen from obscure screenwriter to the top job as head of production. He left when Jack Warner did not fulfill his promise to restore salaries slashed during the depression days.

Jack Warner's actions were always based on his policy that the name Warner Brothers was more important than anyone hired by the studio. To lose a man of Zanuck's ability could have proven disastrous, yet over the years almost every important contract player became embroiled in some sort of a dispute with Warner.

He was the master of the *mal mot*. When I worked on the Warner Brothers lot, he always had the same gag whenever we met. "Oscar," he would say, "you're driving me Wilde." Then he would show his teeth under his moustache, laugh, and flip the ash off his high-priced cigar. It drove *me* wild after a while, but what could I say?

Al Jolson was at the same studio in 1932 and suffered under the same wit. One morning he was indiscreet enough to tell Jack, in no uncertain terms, what he could do with himself. An hour later he had a check buying up his contract, and he was off the lot. That surprised me because Warner usually worked on the principle of George M. Cohan, the famous song and dance man. When Cohan was a producer, he interviewed an actor for a role and finally dismissed him. After the door closed, he told an assistant: "I hate that rat. Remind me never to hire him again unless we need him."

Jack Warner had two rules for actors to observe: No loud ties and no yawns. The last rule based on the premise, I suppose, that a yawn could affect an entire audience.

A picture I did at Warners, *Romance on the High Seas,* was directed by Michael Curtiz. It launched Doris Day. And drydocked me.

When Warner let Mike Curtiz form his own company, Mike signed only one actress to a personal contract. Then he got worried. "Suppose she turns out to be a lesbian?" he asked.

Curtiz liked realism in his movies. For one scene with Errol Flynn playing his customary athletic part, Curtiz had the extras throw real spears. Errol, leaping from turret to turret, felt the true threat of danger as the spears whizzed by. In a rage, he started down the balustrade after the director.

"Lunch!" yelled Curtiz as he ran out the door.

For those early movies, I usually stayed at the Beverly Wilshire Hotel. No matter what city I was in, my attire was always the same. A rumpled blue suit.

One day, I was seated at a table by the pool. I wanted to order a sandwich, but the waiter announced haughtily that he could only serve people in bathing suits. I got up and walked away, but not before I remarked that I wasn't going to undress for any waiter.

The late Louis B. Mayer disliked such productions as John Huston's *Red Badge of Courage,* based on the Civil War story by Stephen Crane. Mayer saw the preview of the picture and loathed it. His comment was: "Here it is, after World War II, and they make a picture with those old rifles, *ping!*"

The head of production then, and the exponent of the "message picture," was Dore Schary. There was great friction between him and L.B., rooted as he was in the old tradition of proven formulae.

Another Schary production that fared even worse was a picture called *The Next Voice You Hear*. In that one, the voice of God was supposed to be heard. Unbelievably, the sound track for God's voice was personally recorded by Dore Schary.

Keenan Wynn, who was at MGM for many years, made a pretty good crack about another producer. "When he laughed, dust came out of his mouth," he said.

During World War II at a large executive luncheon in the MGM commissary, L. B. Mayer rose to his feet at the end of the meal. "Gentlemen," he said solemnly, "a toast to our great President!"

Everyone stood up. L.B. raised his glass. "To Nicholas M. Schenck," he announced.

Nick Schenck, the president of MGM, was on one of his infrequent visits to Hollywood. He was then a very considerable power.

After I finished *An American in Paris* in 1951, I received a letter from Schenck praising my performance. I was pleased of course, but in my usual careless manner I neglected to answer it.

When we met in New York some years later, he still remembered what he called my "insult" and bawled me out for it. He also informed me that he wrote very few complimentary letters to actors. Of course he was perfectly right; I was discourteous. But how could I tell him that the only letters I wrote in years were directed at James Petrillo, trying to get back into the Musicians Union?

Jimmy Dean, the young actor who was a teen-age idol and was killed long before he reached his real potential, once spent a night until five in the morning talking to me about himself and his world. At that time he was working on his biggest picture, *Giant,* with Elizabeth Taylor. Arthur Loew, Jr., brought him to our house, along with Elizabeth, Michael Wilding, Joan Collins, and the producer of *Giant,* Henry Ginsberg. Arthur knew that one of my daughters was an ardent Jimmy Dean fan.

It was a strange thing, but seeing my daughter's room, filled with dozens of pictures of him in various poses, did not seem to please Dean. On the contrary, it depressed him. He said he felt crushed under the weight of such adulation.

He turned out to be a fascinating and intelligent young man who talked fluently about artists in music. And he was surprisingly knowledgeable about such recondite composers as Schoenberg and Bartók.

After James Dean's tragic death a novel was published called *The Immortal,* a thinly disguised story of Dean. The above evening was described in detail—even to what he drank (milk). The author was unknown to me; how he got his information remains a mystery.

I was crazy about the picture *East of Eden*—I still see it on the late show. In that movie, the scenes between the son, Dean, and the father, Raymond Massey, were outstanding. Director Elia Kazan had Dean deliberately antagonize Massey off screen. Massey was outraged by Dean's conduct and resented him deeply. The hostility was transferred to his portrayal, and Kazan achieved the desired effect.

Incidentally, I was told by Nick Ray—the director of *Rebel Without a Cause*—that he had set up a date for Dean with a psychoanalyst, but he was killed in his motorcycle accident three days before the appointment.

Elizabeth Taylor is always a bride, never a bridesmaid. Her five husbands have absolutely nothing in common—except her— their backgrounds and personalities are not consonant. Never has a girl had such a variety of men. The popular belief that a person follows the same pattern, repeats the same mistakes, goes for the same type, seems not to apply to Elizabeth.

Her third marriage to the dynamic showman, Mike Todd, gave her maturity, broadened her periphery. She made the transition from girl to woman—not always an easy thing for an actress to do.

After Mike's tragic death in a plane crash, she grieved deeply. "I should have been on that plane," she confided inconsolably.

For a long while after that, Elizabeth only appeared in public with her old friend Arthur Loew, Jr. Naturally there was speculation as to whether or not they would develop a romance. Especially the night when Arthur gave a dinner party at his home. During the prolonged cocktail hour he suddenly called for attention—he said he had an announcement to make. There was a quick silence—this is *it,* we thought. He smiled at Elizabeth. She smiled at him. "Dinner is served," he announced blandly.

The next time we met, Elizabeth told us that she had decided to go to Europe and visit her friend Noel Coward. She was hoping the trip would not be too painful—her last time there had been with Todd.

On her way to Europe she stopped over in New York. It was then that she and Eddie Fisher ran into each other. They renewed their friendship—then rearranged it. And everyone knows what happened after that. Anyway, she never got to Europe.

When the Eddie-Debbie-Liz thing was the talk of the country, I was doing my TV show in Los Angeles. In an attempt to minimize the scandal I think I compounded it when I said publicly, "Sarah Bernhardt had an illegitimate son, and no one complained about *her.*"

Eddie called me up and said, *"Please*—stop defending us!"

They invited me to a party during their highly publicized courtship. One of the guests was Elizabeth's second husband and father of her two sons, Michael Wilding. Through all of the events that followed—Eddie's divorce from Debbie Reynolds, the marriage of Elizabeth and Eddie, then the Liz-Eddie-

Dick scandal, the divorce of Elizabeth and Eddie, the marriage of Elizabeth and Richard Burton—the only ex-husband who remained on good terms with her was Wilding.

Her first husband, Nick Hilton, made an attempt to renew their relationship after Mike Todd's death. Elizabeth confided that she was not interested.

When I first met her on the MGM lot, she was a teen-age, baby-voice girl appearing in the movie *Little Women*. There was no indication then that she would become the highest paid and most publicized actress in the world. Punished by the movie industry because of her first scandal, she lost the Academy Award for *Suddenly, Last Summer* when she deserved it. She literally almost had to die to be forgiven. The year that Elizabeth won her first award for *Butterfield 8*, Shirley MacLaine had been a strong contender for her role in *The Apartment*.

Said Shirley, "I lost to a tracheotomy."

When Elizabeth won her second Academy Award for *Who's Afraid of Virginia Woolf?* she was criticized for not attending the event.

Yet Richard Burton was responsible for her last-minute change of plan. They were in North Africa, he was not free to accompany her, and he had a dream that her plane crashed. Elizabeth, remembering Mike Todd's fatal air accident, complied with her husband's request and canceled out.

The Academy Awards Show, once a glittering monarchy, has now become a colonial outpost of Santa Monica. At the 1967 one the disparity in the generations was evidenced by the joint appearance of Wendy Hiller and Julie Christie—the regal gown and the mini-skirt, the stately demeanor and the groovy look. I like Olivia de Havilland, but on that Academy Awards Show she oozed such sweetness and warmth she reminded me of a Gentile Molly Berg.

I was rooting for James Mason to win for *Georgy Girl*. His

career is in high gear again. The picture *Lolita* had been a turning point for him.

James was a successful English movie actor when he and his wife Pamela came to New York in the early forties. They issued a statement voicing their disapproval of Hollywood and announced that they planned to live in the East. After a disastrous play they changed their minds.

James was—and is—a very handsome, enigmatic person. He told me that his voice (distinctive though it is) was not strong enough for the theater. When the play had tried out in Philadelphia, a member of the audience got up on the stage and shouted: "James Mason, you stink!" That disturbance made the front pages. Naturally, it left James very wretched.

Ironically, when the Masons did come to Southern California, they became more Hollywood (in the accepted meaning of eccentric, exhibitionistic, etc.) than the natives. Over the years the unconventional manner in which they lived and raised their children, the success and gradual descent of his career, and the preoccupation with hers all added to the general impression.

James always received more acclaim for parts like Rommel in *The Desert Fox,* the spy valet in *Five Fingers,* and the heavy in *North by Northwest,* than he did in leading-man-type roles. When he was offered a secondary part in one particular biblical picture, he was undecided about whether to take it. His wife Pamela suggested, "Tell them you'll only do it if they let *you* be crucified."

After their marriage was over, James returned to Europe. An actor's work, to be effectual, can no longer be rooted in Hollywood—the action is everywhere.

On a return visit James went on TV and talked about his career. His personal choice of all his films was the early *Odd Man Out,* but with his usual British restraint he admitted that he rather liked *Lolita.*

As for the disastrous film *Lord Jim,* fortunately, he said, he only appeared in the last third of the picture—by that time most of the audience had fled.

In the picture *Georgy Girl,* I liked actress Charlotte Rampling, who played the little swinger—to quote somebody's quote, "she clawed her way into my heart." And if you remember the movie, she also played the violin in the symphony orchestra—that makes her a fellow musician.

Richard Harris, the fractious Irish actor, has been mentioned as a possibility for the screen version of *Dylan,* the play about the great Welsh poet Dylan Thomas. Harris had flown from London to New York for one day, expressly to see the New York stage performance with Alec Guinness in the title role. Despite the fact that Guinness was too old and entirely wrong for the character, he gave an absolutely marvelous portrayal. When I commented on this to Richard Harris we found ourselves in agreement.

Harris, who worked in *Mutiny on the Bounty,* the costly picture that almost bankrupted MGM, did not see eye to eye with the star Marlon Brando. Nor did Trevor Howard, I understand.

By the time the premiere came around, there had been so many cuts and revisions that the many actors involved were unaware of what was left in the final version.

Harris did not attend the showing, but his friend Robert Mitchum did. Afterward, Bob called him up.

"You don't have to worry," he reported. "You were the one that everyone was talking about."

They must have left in all of my scenes, thought Harris. But he was quickly deflated.

"Everyone kept asking, 'Which one was Richard Harris?' " was Bob's next remark.

When I met Harris, he affirmed the rumor that his Rolls Royce (the current status symbol) is longer than that of the Queen of England's!

✿   ✿   ✿

The old law of human nature always holds: Do something nice for somebody and they hate you. This is especially pertinent in the case of David Lean, the director, and Noel Coward. In Coward's big years, when he was making such fine pictures as *In Which We Serve* and *Brief Encounter,* Coward selected as his assistant a young man named David Lean. Coward taught him a great deal of his very knowledgeable cinemaship. In *Encounter,* for example, a very poignant love story is heightened immeasurably by being told against the most meager backgrounds, and a Rachmaninoff concerto forms the accompaniment throughout. The whole was very satisfying.

But times change. Now Coward is not precisely popular. His methods are considered old hat, and his technique is out. But David Lean is on top of the heap as a director with such pictures as *Bridge on the River Kwai, Lawrence of Arabia,* and *Dr. Zhivago* to his credit. I asked a friend of both whether Lean would give Coward a job these days. He replied: "Not for a million pounds. You never hire helping hands out of your past." I have no idea if this is true, but it sounds like human nature.

In Noel Coward's initial production of *Private Lives* his understudy was one John Gielgud. And the role of the stuffy husband was played realistically by Laurence Olivier.

The first American movie that Olivier ever did, I believe, was *Queen Christina* with Greta Garbo—but he never appeared in it. He had worked only two weeks on the set when he was pulled off and replaced by John Gilbert. For a long while it was believed that Garbo's affection for Gilbert had something to do with his replacement. Even so, Olivier was so humiliated that he refused to talk about it for years. When he felt he had finally atoned for his disgrace, he confessed that he "did not have the weight at the time." He was not speaking about avoirdupois, and he was right.

Apropos of Greta Garbo, I was once dining at Le Pavillon

when the inaccessible actress came in. I called the headwaiter over and said, "Please tell Miss Garbo to quit staring at me."

He told her; she laughed and invited me to join her. She was cheerfully drinking a martini with her escort. I explained I was leaving for Emporia, Kansas, to play a concert.

"Why don't you come with me?" I added.

"What time does the train arrive?" she inquired.

"Eleven in the morning," I said.

"Ah, too late for breakfast," she pronounced.

One of the better New York restaurants is Le Pavillon, where most of the successful people have dined at one time or another. It was under the tyrannical one-man rule of the late Henri Soule, who ran it as his own dictatorship. Soule usually won his battles with his customers, but one of the most dramatic went by decision to Harry Cohn, head of Columbia Studios. The great man was finally convinced by one of his Hollywood courtiers that Le Pavillon was the place to go and be seen, not only for its great food but also for its publicity value. Cohn went and was duly seated—as he said later, "some place back in the bleachers near the kitchen." He declared that he felt stifled, surrounded as he was by "arguing waiters and dirty dishes."

Cohn demanded to see Soule to complain. Of course, he never was accorded that privilege. He stamped out in a fury after a meal that was, to him, totally unsatisfactory. On the way out, he managed one pregnant sentence with Soule: "I'm going to look into your rent."

Unfortunately for Soule, Columbia Pictures owned the building in which he was situated. The Cohn incident eventually cost Soule twice his yearly $17,500 rent. He also lost his wine basement. Cohn preempted it for storing old Columbia film cans.

During the Communist cabal in Hollywood, Cohn had a talented producer running the studio. The producer always had a stooge following him around.

Finally Cohn warned the producer, "You'd better get rid of that fellow. I think he's a Communist."

But the producer refused. The stooge turned out to be an FBI agent, and the producer was turned in. The spot identification of anyone as a Communist has never been less reliable.

Rita Hayworth was the biggest star discovery of Harry Cohn. After her divorce from Aly Khan, she resumed her picture career and, with her two children, moved to Beverly Hills.

My daughter Amanda, then about ten, came home one day with the giggles.

"There's a little kid across the street on roller skates, and she says that she's a princess!"

It was Yasmin, the daughter of Rita and Aly Khan, and she really *was* a princess.

Yasmin was driven to school in a car pool with other children. On one ride the chatter went like this:

"I'm a Catholic."

"So am I."

"I'm Jewish."

"So am I."

Yasmin turned to her nurse. "What am I?" she whispered. The nurse whispered back.

"I'm a Moslem," announced Yasmin. She waited for the echo. When there was none, she turned to her nurse. "I don't want to be a Moslem," she complained. "Nobody else is."

Naturally she was too young to know that there are several hundred million other Moslems, even if they aren't in Beverly Hills.

Another time Amanda came home from school and announced that she had received the second highest grade in her class.

"Wonderful!" we assured her. "Who was first?"

"Max Factor," she replied.

"What's that old man doing in your class?" I asked.

I was relieved to find out that she meant Max Factor III.

The only advice I ever got from any director in a dozen films was not to put my hand in front of my face.

Otto Preminger is a highly successful producer-director, of course, but he has an intimidating Prussian personality. During the shooting of one of his pictures, an actor nervously fluffed his lines, then fluffed them again. Preminger sprang out of his director's chair like a bull elephant from ambush and roared: *"Relax!"* It got quite a reaction but not the one he expected.

It was Preminger who recently had a disagreement with the Little Napoleon of agents, Irving Lazar (whom I once described as the Jewish Onassis of Beverly Hills—the only man to ride down Wilshire Boulevard in a yacht). The fracas with Preminger ended when Irving abruptly broke a glass over Preminger's billiard-bald head on the principle, I suppose, of anything to make a point. It left Preminger dripping with cold blood—and with a slash that took forty-eight stitches and a lawsuit to heal. I told Preminger that now they could use a closeup of his head as a picture of the landscape of the moon.

One time I saw Otto in a restaurant, eating with a writer named Sy Bartlett. I stopped by the table to say hello to him. I then turned to Bartlett and decided to be nice. "Sy," I said, "you're looking wonderful."

"Oscar!" cried Otto in disbelief. "That's the first *witless* thing I ever heard you say!"

That's what I got for trying to change my image.

I was told about the Broadway play *Will Success Spoil Rock Hunter?*, in which the late Jayne Mansfield had her first important role. The morning after the opening, Jayne swept into the office of the producer.

"I'm a star!" she exclaimed. "I feel marvelous!"

"Have you read the reviews?" asked the producer.

"What reviews?" she demanded.

The producer handed her the papers. She slowly read what the critics had to say. At last she looked up. "What does 'inept' mean?" she asked softly.

The author of the above play as well as many Hollywood movies is George Axelrod. I met him before the play was produced, at his home in New York. He was a nervous, fast-talking young man, and he was telling me about the problems he was confronted with in regard to casting, theater, etc. In the middle of his long-winded monologue, I began searching around for a cigarette. George absent-mindedly took a cigarette out of his pack, lit it up, and handed it to me.

"But I'm not in love with you," I said as I accepted it with surprise.

I remarked once to Harry Kurnitz, the writer and poker player, at a time when Leopold Stokowski with his wonderful hands and white mane of hair was at his peak of popularity, that "there's a play in that man." Harry had lived in Philadelphia, so he was well-acquainted with the maestro's idiosyncrasies. Not too long after, allowing for the normal processes of creative gestation, Harry came out with the successful comedy *Once More, with Feeling*.

It was Kurnitz who took the train from Los Angeles to New York for the express purpose of spending three uninterrupted days resting, reading, and sleeping. The first night out, in order to insure a good start, he took what he thought were two sleeping pills. Unfortunately for him they were Dexedrine tablets—he was awake and jumping most of the trip.

Getting Hollywood to be classically music conscious has been part of my lifework. I once took a producer with me to a Beethoven festival because I thought I might educate him. He went because he wanted to enhance his status as a thinker. He sat through it all, but he was obviously relieved when the last number came up. It was Beethoven's C Minor Symphony, which is distinguished by a number of false climaxes. At the first he got up, and, as the orchestra continued, he sank back. At the second he did the same thing. And at the third he tensed and relaxed, then turned to me.

"The louse fooled me again," he said apologetically.

The phrase that I think was invented by Oscar Wilde, "Don't shoot the piano player, he's doing the best he can," might be applied to what happens to pianists in the movies. They do their jobs, but they are always shot the same way. Usually they open up with a very big closeup of the twinkling hands of the player (always with a mirror where the piano trademark ought to be), then they pull back slowly into a decreasingly dramatic long shot showing him surrounded either by massed musicians or (if he is in love) nothing at all. I claim the responsibility for suggesting an entirely new shot: I reversed it so that at the climax of the piece the camera came in from a very long shot and ended on my hands. I did this when I played a truncated version of some Tchaikovsky in *The Barkleys of Broadway.*

For the "ego fantasy" scene in *American in Paris,* I played the last movement of the Gershwin Concerto. It was recorded, as usual, before the actual scene was filmed. When I was well into the number my eye fell on a discarded candy bar wrapper lying on the floor—the words "Butter Finger" stared up at me—not exactly an inspiration for a pianist to behold! Averting my gaze, I managed to finish the piece—saved by my customary frenzied composure.

In the thirties and forties, the great house for all German refugees in Southern California was that of Salka Viertel, the mother of the screenwriter (and Deborah Kerr's husband) Peter Viertel. All Germans who got past Ellis Island in those days made a beeline for hospitality at the Viertels.

One of these refugees was Dmitri Tiomkin—now well known

as a Hollywood composer. But in those remote times, Tiomkin was having a very hard time getting any work at all as a composer, much less a picture to score. He bemoaned his plight to Salka. She compassionated him. "Dmitri," she said comfortingly, "that is the way of all genius. I can prove it. Take my husband, Berthold, who is a *real* genius."

I have no idea if Dmitri felt comforted. I know that years afterward he appeared on my TV program, and I asked him if he was an "epigone in music." He said he was. Then, hours after the show was taped, he called up and demanded that the whole twenty-five minutes be excised. I guess he had thought it over in the meantime. It means "a collector from every source."

The advice I got on my music was another thing. I did the score for one production with a Parisian background. The producer heard it. I waited for his response. "It's good, Oscar," he said around his cigar, "but it's not Frenchy enough."

"All right," I said grudgingly. "I'll put in some more French horns."

The six months I spent in Hollywood in 1929 just before the Crash were the wildest months I ever dissipated in my misspent life. It was a wide-open era. Everybody who was anyone used to either stay or amuse themselves at the Roosevelt Hotel on Hollywood Boulevard—which was then a lot less cluttered by people, cars, and buildings, and possessed a good deal more scenery. The Garden of Allah was still a hot place; so was the famous old defunct Hollywood Hotel at Hollywood and Highland.

One night there was a dance at the Roosevelt Hotel, and Ben Gimbel of the department store family was present. I took a dislike to Ben, probably because I thought he was trying to make my date. I hit him. I did not actually hit him, of course— I had my hands to think of; I got up behind him and pushed him so that he fell over a table, which in his condition was easy to do.

What I did not know then—and which if I did would have
man. Bill was the tough director who came back from flying
prevented my action—was that he was a close friend of Bill Well-
in World War I with shrapnel in his jaw and, for all I know,
some in his fists. Wellman came up to me and said menacingly:
"So you're a one-punch guy, eh?"

All I could think of in my desperation was that I would
get killed. I had not figured on Wellman's being a friend of
Ben. *My* rage had subsided, but evidently Wellman-Gimbel
were still mad. I just hoped that Wellman would get the execution over with as soon as possible.

We stepped outside and circled around and exchanged a few
token punches. Then, in the nick of time, as they say, the
friends that I was frantically beckoning to broke it up. Ben
and I later became very good friends.

Those months were Babylon in person. William Le Baron,
who was in charge at RKO, had hired me to write music. Since
RKO had just been put in competition, it got all the dregs of
the songwriting world. I, it seemed, had been hired to raise
the tone of the establishment. That was the first mistake of
many in RKO's career, but Howard Hughes was the only other
big one.

Long before Irene Dunne was appointed as an ambassadress
to the United Nations she used her diplomacy in a different way
when we were a team at RKO. When the visiting exhibitors
would tour the studio, we would pander to their finer sensibilities. I would play and Irene would sing. Irene not only became
an expert comedienne; she and Rex Harrison played *Anna and
the King of Siam,* a memorable movie, long before it was made
into the musical, *The King and I.*

My job had a lot of facets and one of the best was picking
the girls to sing the songs I wrote. I will not say that I romanced
all of them but I certainly tried.

I helped start George Raft on his movie career. He was in a

line of extras when I suggested to the assistant director that he be given a few lines of dialogue.

Raft went on to a real success in the movies. He was offered many good roles but turned down many of them because he thought they would tarnish his image. This when he was reported to be an off-screen friend of members of the mob! But the Raft refusals had a good outcome: they helped the career of Humphrey Bogart. Raft was a very gentle guy, despite his tough reputation. I never saw him hit anyone, but Johnny Broderick, the tough cop and Broadway hero, always hated him. I guess Raft stole the limelight too often. Johnny Broderick was a friend of mine who judged people by a handshake. He estimated their character and personality by the strength of their grip. He shook hands with me once. I had to cancel half a concert season because of his estimate. They made a picture about Broderick's life called *Ballots and Bullets,* which starred Edward G. Robinson. Eddie smoked a cigar during some scenes. Broderick's comment on it was a bellow of pain.

"What are my kids going to think?" he demanded. "I never smoked a cigar in my life! Did any of you guys see me smoke a cigar?"

Frank Costello, who supposedly ran the rackets in New York for years, always had a little more of my sympathy than Broderick. At a meeting of the Kefauver Senate committee investigating crime, Costello, appearing as a witness, said on the stand: "You believe a bum like Broderick but you won't believe me."

That night there was a gang in Toots Shor's restaurant expectantly waiting for the showdown between Costello and Broderick. Costello showed, all right. Broderick never put in an appearance. It lost him some friends.

One had to be careful in dealing with some of those characters. There was a famous gangster who made a habit of greeting his friends by knuckling them on the forehead—sometimes rather painfully. I was sitting at a table in a restaurant one night, engrossed in my dinner, when I was knuckled. I leaped up and started a punch. Then I saw who had knuckled me. I changed the punch in midair to an embrace. My scowl turned to a smile.

Edward G. Robinson, who despite his tough screen roles must have been the prototype for the song, "Dear Hearts and Gentle People," had difficulty in an early picture with George Raft. Eddie, an experienced stage actor with a skillful technique, was viewed with distrust by Raft, a movie personality of limited acting range.

In scenes together, Raft would stop the scene and angrily accuse Eddie of acting.

"I caught you—you did it again—stop *acting!*"

All this must have been pretty hard for Eddie to take, as ludicrous as it may sound now. But time has taken good care of Eddie Robinson—he has earned the respect that his accomplishments, and his years, command.

There must be a moral to be drawn from the fact that some of the biggest draws in the early days of motion pictures were ugly stars. Think of Wallace Beery, Percy Kilbride, Marjorie Main, and Marie Dressler for starters.

One of the facts that surprised me about Wally Beery was that he was in the same class with Edward Everett Horton at Columbia University. In my image of Beery, I never imagined he even got near elementary school.

I recall Charlie Chaplin, for instance, very well. I agree that he was an accomplished actor and a comedy genius on the screen, but I found him rather tedious off. Conversationally, he was a one-man cadenza. I once asked him if he was ever jealous of any other actor.

"Yes," Chaplin said, "I was jealous of Lloyd Hamilton." Hamilton was a very fat, very funny comedian who died very young. He is forgotten now.

It was in those precrash days that I remember going to a party at Jack Pickford's. It was the best fun in the world, it seemed, at those movie orgies, to throw the furniture through closed windows. It made a satisfactory sound and mess and always climaxed any successful movie party. One girl passed out cold, and I drove her six miles to her apartment. When we got there, she revived and said: "Live with me awhile." So I found out that the peacemaker is blessed.

I met one great beauty who was a semistar in Hollywood and sat next to her at dinner.

"I'm sorry they sat me next to you," I said apologetically. She immediately became furious. She was a little dull anyway, and whereas I meant that I felt she should have a better companion, she felt that I meant I was doomed to her company.

After that we fell in love and had a romance. She worried about her face all the time. The one thing I got out of our love was a bill for damages to my car. It seems that another movie personality was in love with her. He was irritated when my car was parked in front. So he deliberately rammed my car, causing a good many dents. At the time, I thought it was a peculiar way of anyone's showing his strength, even though I sympathized with his mood.

Some years later my girl married a great movie star. She divorced him and went to England and married a title. But I had discovered that sex to certain English women is like oatmeal for kids—marriage for them is often just an operation base for infidelity.

When I was young, I used to do an act at private parties that was like fortune-telling on the piano. I would create a characterization in music. Someone might ask me to sit down at the keyboard and improvise a personality, and I would oblige. Clare Boothe Luce once asked me to sketch her in notes, and I created a tiny glissando. When I noted that she indulged in intellectual baby talk, she became slightly upset.

However, Clare was always capable of speaking my mind. I remarked to her some years ago, "I guess Greer Garson doesn't know whether to choose between her marriage or her career." To which Clare replied: "Soon she won't have a choice."

Years ago I had a date with Lucille Ball, who was then a beautiful chorine. A friend told me that a certain photographer had taken her out and made a pass at her. "What did she do?" I asked, always interested in such matters.

"She pulled a gun on him," my friend said seriously.

That night I met Lucille at the door for our date. "I'm sorry, Lucille," I said to her, "but I'll have to frisk you before I take you out."

When I met Mia Farrow, I said to her, "I know your mother was brought over to this country from Ireland for a John McCormick movie." Her mother, Maureen O'Sullivan, was one of the beautiful girls I used to go out with. I knew she was a lady, and I treated her with all the respect that such a condition demands. McCormick, the great Irish singer, had been imported to Hollywood as the Irish answer to Jewish Al Jolson, but as it happened he did not make the grade.

It is not enough to say that ego drives a movie star. It has to be something deeper than that, a compulsion of the personality to keep going. I remember that when Joan Fontaine married Brian Aherne, she told him she was going to give up her career. Then David Selznick offered her the script for *Rebecca*. She couldn't resist such a wonderful part. She told Brian, "Just this one picture and that's *all*." She won the Academy Award, her career went on, and her marriage was down the drain. She later said that for the first thirty days she was always afraid she would be fired—but this is not an uncommon fear among actors.

A few years ago I was seated next to Joan Fontaine at a big dinner party. She is a lovely actress and a beautiful woman. We had an interesting talk, and she asked me to dance with her. "Sorry," I said. "I wish that I could. But if I dance with you, I have to dance with my wife. And I haven't the strength for two dances."

A far-out conversational opening came from Debbie Power Loew, the wife of the late actor Tyrone Power. Seated by me at a dinner party, she turned and said: "I prefer your Beethoven to your Schnabel." What could I answer? I choked up for most of the evening.

Although June used to be on the stage and has returned to acting, actresses as a group have never particularly fascinated me. And some actresses never manage the transfer from a little girl to a woman. Jeanne Crain was one of them, and I always liked her. On one occasion when we did a movie together I kissed her so hard that she fell down in the street. She is still beautiful, which reminds me of when I met conductor Vladimir Golschmann's wife the first time. "You've been a famous beauty for years," I remarked. I meant it as a compliment—it just came out wrong.

Nowadays, I somehow manage always to say the wrong things to women. I encountered Natalie Wood, who is rich, free, beautiful, and young. "If I were forty years younger," I began— "I'd be too young for you," I concluded.

Things change so fast in the movie industry that I was not surprised to hear that prospective tenants are now being shown "the *old* George Segal house."

One recent night I saw *The Diary of Anne Frank* on television; the next night I saw *The Shop on Main Street* in the movie theater—quite a lot for a Jew to sit through in eighteen hours!

So I am seeing new movies less and watching old movies more. In response to the question as to what picture I have enjoyed lately, I reply without hesitation: *Springtime in the Rockies,* with Betty Grable and Cesar Romero.

Chapter 6

*M*USICAL tours are always terrors. They are not always made easier by one's assistants. I had a man who tried to smooth the path of my wanderings through the hinterlands, but he was a very ineffectual bastard. I made it worse by saying to him, "Everybody makes mistakes." Ever afterward, when he made a botch of what he was doing, he would quote my words of wisdom back at me. "I know people make mistakes sometimes!" I bellowed at last. "But not *all* of the time." He never believed it.

The worst remark I ever heard about concert music came to my ear at a university in Florida. I was there to play a concert. As my encore, I indulged in "Malaguena," an attractive cheap composition that I had made into a best-selling record. As I finished and the audience wanted more, the dean whispered in my ear: "Can't you give them something lighter?"

I was struck with astonishment. Asking for a lighter piece than "Malaguena" is like asking someone to find something lighter than a helium balloon. Which reminds me of the time I gave a concert in Miami, Florida. I couldn't practice at the hotel in the daytime, as I was told it disturbed the guests.

My friend, the late George Solitaire, was incensed by this edict. He protested to the manager: "Your guests make more noise *eating* than Levant does practicing!"

Time after time, concerts and recitals are interrupted by latecomers. On one occasion when I was in the middle of a number, a bejeweled matron came sweeping down the aisle, distracting the audience. I stopped my performance of a Poulenc piece and began choreographing her walk by playing in time with her steps. She hesitated and slowed down—I slowed down. She stopped—I stopped. She hurried—I hurried. By the time she reached her seat, the audience was in hysterics and the matron in a state of wild confusion. I don't know if it cured her tardiness, but it gave me a routine to use on other inconsiderate arrivals.

One time when I played Indianapolis, I was the dinner guest of the head of the Eli B. Lilly Company. The organization makes among other things Seconal, Tuonol, and Amytal. The president had been an English doctor. He showed me his paintings—the best collection of old masters in the United States, excluding the two coasts.

Then he asked, "Is there anything you want?"

"Nothing," I said, "but what would you advise me to take?"

He replied, "Take Eli Lilly's vitamin pills and Seconal."

It was wasted on me then. If he would only ask me now!

When I played with the symphony at Salt Lake City in the tabernacle there, the Mormon sponsors asked me not to smoke in their church. I told them that I would desist. When, during the performance, someone suggested that we sneak a smoke, I refused. I would not even smoke in the tabernacle grounds; I did not scratch a match until we left the gates—which exit was a relief. But I respected their courtesy as much as their creed.

The only helpful advice I got from a critic was when I played Cincinnati. He suggested that I bring out the bass notes more emphatically in the *Moonlight Sonata*—advice that I followed.

In that city, I met a concert manager who told me an interesting story about Leopold Stokowski. In the early 1900's Mrs. Taft, of the famous Cincinnati family, went to Europe to hire a conductor for the city orchestra. An unknown organist by the name of Leo Stokes, employed at a cathedral in New York, heard about Mrs. Taft's mission, went to Paris, and hired an orchestra for half of a program in order to present himself as a candidate. He was chosen after the competition had narrowed down to him and Bruno Walter. He then adopted the name Stokowski, and during his first year in Cincinnati, newspapers made a point of spelling his name phonetically. Enormously gifted, handsome, and eminently successful, he married his first wife Olga Samaroff (née Hickenlooper), an accomplished American pianist who bore him two children. Stokowski eventually went on to Philadelphia, where as everyone knows, he molded that orchestra into a magnificent institution.

Not many people recall it, perhaps, but I played my first concert at the Hollywood Bowl in 1929. The *pièce de résistance* was something called *A March for Two Pianos and Orchestra* by Robert Russell Bennett, with Bennett and me at the two pianos. We felt sure it would be a hit, so we spent a good deal of time rehearsing our bows. But the conductor, a man named Karl Krueger, messed up the ending, and we took no bows at all. It was a great disappointment.

By 1951 things were quite different. That was the year when the Hollywood Bowl, because of a lack of public interest, had to cancel its season after two disastrous weeks. The old management was out, and Mrs. Dorothy Chandler, wife of the owner of the Los Angeles *Times,* took charge.

She asked me to play a Gershwin concert, the proceeds to be used for financing a revised schedule. I was glad to extend my services, the concert sold out, and the Bowl was back in business. (I never got a nickel for that performance but then I did not ask for a nickel.)

One summer at Robin Hood Dell in Philadelphia, some myopic publicist ran a huge banner across the entrance. It read: MITROPOULOS–FUCHS– and I forget the name of the third. The first two sufficed to keep the audience in a state of mild hysteria for most of the season.

Another spot that was not exactly inspiring to touring musicians was Des Moines, Iowa. One winter Vladimir Horowitz asked me where I would open my tour. I told him: "Des Moines."

Horowitz rolled his eyes upward in sympathy. "Dostoevski!" he groaned commiseratingly.

It should be said that one of Horowitz's great achievements was in popularizing his name. Before his time, no one with a name like that had dared to use it for concerts. They sometimes used a pseudonym or altered it—like Josef Lhévinne whose name is really Levine but who added enough additional letters to Frenchify it. Horowitz made his last name sound good because *he* was so good that he sanctified it.

Lately Horowitz has overcome his multitude of fears and appears once more in public. During his twelve-year hiatus he made piano recordings at home, thereby prompting Eugene Ormandy, conductor of the Philadelphia Symphony Orchestra, to jestingly say that he would be glad to record with Horowitz if he could squeeze a hundred men into his living room.

On my 1964 trip to New York I was invited by Horowitz to

his home—it was the only time that we had seen each other during the years of his voluntary retirement. Previous to that and because of his sensitivity, I hadn't wanted to subject him to my own malaise.

He was in good health, still looking boyish in spite of his age, and I discovered that he practiced faithfully every day for hours.

During the evening he pointed silently at a bare wall that had at one time been hung with two impressionist paintings. Obviously his dozen years of inactivity had caused a monetary drain.

The question of resuming his career after such a prolonged absence presented many problems to one of the world's foremost virtuosos. Not only had a whole new generation of pianists emerged, several possessing technical brilliance never before heard (although the level of expressivity diminishes with every decade), but his own repertory had become somewhat outmoded. However, it was the memory of his brilliant career that posed the biggest threat. "I am frightened by my own legend," he confessed.

Yet he had to return to the concert hall. I knew that, because it is always the live audience that makes the great performance. Television, radio, records, tapes—all these are fine but never enough. The real artist finds that the difference—the inspiration of tempi, nuance, and expression—comes from the rise and ebb of spirit between performer and people. Horowitz likes people, but he cannot always manage the language except in his own mysterious way. A generation or so ago he met Mrs. Herbert Hoover, wife of the President of the United States. "I am delightful," he said, bowing.

My wife also cherishes an autographed picture that was warmly inscribed to her thus: To June, from his sincere admirer, V. Horowitz.

Early in his career, Horowitz, whose stage decorum is impeccable, was appalled by the advice given him by the distinguished pianist Artur Schnabel: "When the piece gets difficult, make faces." Needless to say, this advice was ignored.

Program making is a very important part of an artist's career. Schnabel, the great specialist, who played all-Beethoven programs, said self-deprecatingly that the difference between him and other pianists who played a variety of works was that his program was not only dull in the first half—it was also dull in the second half.

But as music critic Virgil Thomson put it: "A program should not consist of all encore pieces."

Schnabel secretly composed music in the twelve-tone or serial system. Arnold Schoenberg, the originator of the system, made a pungent comment about Schnabel's music: "His compositions never have a one-beat or one-bar rest in the whole work." He was right. Schnabel's process is like the Xerox process; it simply goes on and on in a sort of assembly-line music. But Schoenberg will last; as he himself said to Virgil Thomson: "My system will assure Germany of musical superiority for the next two hundred years."

In the thirties, when I was studying with Schoenberg, he asked me to be his assistant at UCLA. I turned it down, as I didn't think I qualified, even though Schoenberg's theory was that a teacher learns from his pupils.

It was at that time that I rather nervously showed George Gershwin a piano piece that I had written under the tutelage of the master. After careful examination, George's reaction was, "It looks so confused!"

"Didn't you know?" I retorted. "I've just been offered the chair of confusion at UCLA."

I shudder to think of the wonderful *chutzpah* I had in those days. *Chutzpah* is pronounced by dropping the *c* and bringing the throat up into the mouth for the rest of the word—and it means that quality which enables a man who has murdered his mother and father to throw himself on the mercy of the court as an orphan. In other words, sheer gall, undiluted brass.

Most of it occurred when I was associated with Schoenberg. I used to go as a total unknown to the meetings of the composers and present my point of view with verve, *élan,* sangfroid, and a loud voice. Each time one of the members would turn around and shout: "Who the hell are you?" But then it is always true that the disciples are more arrogant than the master.

When I studied with Schoenberg, I wrote a piano concerto. It was in three movements. I wanted to make it palatable to popular taste so I inserted a boogie-woogie strain in the middle of it. It spoiled the whole thing. That is the usual fate of jazz; it becomes more and more dated.

Two of my formal pieces were conducted by the concertmaster for the Boston Symphony. I came away in the depths of depression. It was a very bad job of exposing to the audience what I had done. For the first time I realized how other composers must feel when their compositional dreams are not realized in execution.

As difficult as it has always been for composers to obtain a first performance of their work, nowadays it is almost impossible for them to get a second performance.

In the late twenties and early thirties, American composing was a dogged, bankrupt affair. It was the tiny Coscob Press of Connecticut, for example, that first published the music of Aaron Copland. The outfit was financed by Alma Wertheim, the wife of the chief backer of the New York Theatre Guild. The Wertheims eventually divorced, and he married an actress, Ruth Warfield. Ruth, with the usual perverseness of the arts, had other ambitions.

"How is your work coming?" I asked her once.

"I'm having trouble with my melodic line," she said blithely. It was hardly the answer I expected. Incidentally, Rossini stopped composing when he was very young, relatively in his prime, and gave a wonderful reason for it.

"When I was young," he said, "the melodies chased me. Now, I have to chase them."

The French composer Erik Satie was one of the most interesting and eccentric personalities of the twenties. He was the man who asserted that "artists have no longer any need to call themselves artists. They may as well leave the term to those who find it glamorous—hairdressers and chiropodists." In 1925 Satie wrote a ballet. Part of it was on film, in which he himself appeared. It showed him firing cannon from various rooftops, supposedly blowing up Paris. The public reaction was both amusement and outrage.

The shaggy-dog variety of nonsense story has never particularly attracted me, but I appreciate one that was told by Satie. It concerned the medieval king who built a marvelously beautiful flight of marble stairs. They were so charming that he barred the proletariat from using them. Then he excluded the nobility, then his personal friends. Only the king was allowed to use the stairs, and finally he barred himself from their use.

"There was only one thing left to do," Satie concluded. "He had them stuffed."

Satie's quixotic direction for a piano piece of his was: *To be played with both hands in the pocket.*

His eccentricities carried over into his personal life. He lived in a part of Paris near a glue factory and never permitted visitors. It was reported that his bedsheets were never changed. They eventually became completely black.

During the aleatory, electronic, Stockhausen phase of music (John Cage, etc.) there was a concert at Judson Hall in New York. Somebody had discovered a piece of Erik Satie's, a very small piece, with the directions: *To be played hundreds of times without pause.* This was faithfully carried out, by having innumerable pianists replacing each other around the clock, and with the audience coming and going at will. It took days.

Debussy was Satie's close friend, and Ravel paid for the publishing of one of Satie's compositions. Ravel, by the way, was the composer who refused membership in the Académie Française. Satie declared, "Ravel refuses, but his music accepts."

Recently I mentioned loudly to a friend that the two greatest composers of the nineteenth century, Beethoven and Brahms, never got married. This was for the benefit of my wife, who was listening. I imitate Brahms in that I never keep anything of a personal nature. Brahms got rid of all his intimate notes—I like him quite well for it.

But my opinion of Brahms is not shared in all quarters. During World War II, the Russians released the Tchaikovsky diaries for publication. In one passage, Tchaikovsky noted that Brahms had praised his Fifth Symphony but had added that the last movement was not up to the standard of the others. Tchaikovsky noted violently: "Brahms is shit!" I discussed this with Virgil Thomson who nodded sagely and said: "Brahms *was* a shit."

I remember discussing conducting with Bernard Herrmann, the movie composer-conductor. Although Beethoven's Fifth Symphony is by now an overplayed work, the famous first four bars are interpreted differently by every conductor.

Asked Bernie: "How would *you* conduct the Beethoven Fifth?"

"I'd skip the first four bars," I replied.

Times have changed. As long ago as 1958 I gave up performing seriously on the piano. Previous to that I had turned out albums literally by the dozen. Over the years I not only recorded eight concerti, but numerous piano works that included Liszt, Debussy, Chopin, and miscellaneous composers. For ten years my record of George Gershwin's *Rhapsody in Blue* was the number one best seller in the classical category.

Of course I became identified with *Rhapsody in Blue* because I played it so often. Nina Foch, the actress, once told me she was born in 1924. "That was a good year," I said. "It produced you and the *Rhapsody*."

In other books I have written of the enormous impact that the *Rhapsody* had when it was first performed in this country; it caused a sensation. It may be interesting, therefore, to learn the reaction of the respected and accomplished pianist Dame Myra Hess. The following is from another letter of Laurence Stallings:

> I was present at Blanche Knopf's when a brilliant young Englishwoman, Myra Hess, first saw the score of *Rhapsody in Blue*. George [Gershwin] brought it there, and the future Dame Myra, while fascinated, was nevertheless slightly appalled, in a well-bred English fashion, at his innovations. She read the middle passages well, however. (And How!) But I continued to think of the line W. S. Gilbert gives Bunthorne in "Patience" which reflects English taste. It was something about the English preference for "a not too-French, French bean."

The stories about George Gershwin and his totally confident opinion about himself are many. Not too well known is the one about the time he took a taxi uptown to see a Columbia football game. The driver wove an arabesque between the supports of the then-elevated railroad. George leaned over and tapped him on the shoulder. "For God's sake, man," he remonstrated, "drive carefully! You've got Gershwin in the car!"

George had the most inventive and personal flair for piano performing—apart from his genius at composition—that I have ever seen. Not that he used flamboyant gestures such as José Iturbi—he was simply a delight to watch, especially when he played his own music, which he usually did. On one occasion Charles Lindbergh sat next to George while he played. He watched him as if hypnotized. George, running off his own pieces, was flattered.

"Do you like music that much?" he asked Lindbergh.

"No," said Lindbergh. "I just like to watch your hands."

Before his tragic illness, George told me of two projects that he had in mind for the future. One was to set the Gettysburg Address to music and the other was to make an opera of *Die Golem,* a macabre Yiddish legend which tells of a rabbi in Prague confecting a mechanical man-monster.

Unhappily, posterity was to be denied these works.

One of the most terrible remarks I ever heard was made recently by Clifton Fadiman. "As time goes by, everything goes," he said mournfully. "Even Gershwin." I can hardly bear to think about that.

All of my professional life I have been a musical ambivalent. I have played popular and classical music with equal gusto—but when I started to play with symphony orchestras I discovered that it was almost a Federal offense to play popular music on the concert stage.

With the exception of one or two very short tours by George Gershwin himself, Gershwin music had never been played on a concert swing. It took more than one hundred and fifty years for this country to begin to become musically sophisticated. When I began to play concerts across the country in the forties, indigenous symphony orchestras were just beginning to crop up. They were uniformly so bad and untrained that my private opinion was that it would be better to have one good orchestra from a large city tour the nation.

Then there seemed to be a musical renaissance, and time proved me to be wrong. There are now numerous fine symphonies throughout the states; we are even developing our own great native conductors.

I care for Leonard Bernstein, who has taken the spotlight from Stokowski, in the way that I would care for a kid brother. But he has a wife who dislikes me. I said to Leonard, "Your wife seems very neurotic about your friends."

"No," Leonard said, "it's just that she has strong opinions." (Especially about me.)

I may have been too harsh with Lenny, criticizing him as much as I have. It was one of those challenges that are so unrewarding.

I think it is amazing how a good line improves with age in the music world. When I met Arnold Schoenberg in 1935, he said to me that I had a "very talented face." I was overcome with pleasure. More than thirty years later, I repeated the same line to Lenny and enjoyed an even higher degree of reaction.

On my last trip to New York, Lenny and I could never quite agree on when to get together though we had the nagging desire. He asked me to lunch with him and I refused: I said I had not had lunch outside the house for six years (as a matter of fact, I have only had one afternoon out in five years). Then he asked me to come to his rehearsal.

"I'd rather see you without your orchestra," I said. He took it as a compliment and came to my hotel. He even guessed my age, making me younger than I really am, which was a rather nice gesture.

I also renewed acquaintance with an old friend, the renowned symphonic trumpet player (now retired) Harry Glanz. I asked him what he thought about Leonard Bernstein. The veteran Glanz considered a few seconds, then said: "Well, he's better than Walter Damrosch." I presume he was thinking about the children's programs that Damrosch initiated.

I told Lenny, who happens to be a protégé of Serge Koussevitzky, that I had heard his mentor conduct the Mahler Ninth as far back as the 1930's.

"How did you like it?" he inquired.

"I was overwhelmed," I said, "but by Mahler, not Koussevitzky." Then I was seized by curiosity.

"Do you identify yourself with Mahler?" I asked Lenny.

"Only when I play Mahler," he said.

"But you play Mahler all the time," I rejoined.

The next season I noticed that he played the Mahler Ninth Symphony to great critical acclaim.

Koussevitzky was prodigal about the future in the sense of providing American music. He accounted for most of the commissions of original works. I think that Koussevitzky left this country a much greater musical legacy than Toscanini. The latter left unsurpassed recordings of great classical music; but Koussevitzky, for his part, commissioned original compositions by Americans almost constantly. He also founded Tanglewood, the traditional summer festival in New England for the benefit of new works and young conductors. It is an invaluable legacy.

Boston held him in the highest regard. Not only because of his long stay there but also because of his imposing presence and musical inspiration, he was a genuine idol. At one reception, a Boston matron came up to him and with awe said: "Mr. Koussevitzky, you are a god to me."

To which Koussevitzky said with the utmost understanding and good humor: "Ah, madam, what a responsibility!"

One pianist who is excellent but who has more eccentricities than most is Glenn Gould. At one of his concerts with the New York Philharmonic, Leonard Bernstein made a preconcert speech in which he said he disagreed with Gould's interpretation of the music, but that he would defend to the death Gould's right to play it as he saw it.

The concerto happened to be the Brahms D Minor. Gould gave a very languid interpretation to this pretentious work, one which I have called "an heroic bore." His rendition established a world's record. It lasted fifteen minutes longer than any previous playing. Afterward Irving Kolodin, the music editor of the *Saturday Review,* asked Gould why he had done it that way. He replied: "I felt very baroque."

Gould has the unusual habit of playing the piano with his legs crossed. He was the one who on the hundredth anniversary of the birth of Richard Strauss wrote a stunning piece for the *Saturday Review*. I had only one objection to it—it was practically all about Mendelssohn. Interestingly enough, he predicted the renaissance of that composer, who is hardly ever played today. When I was a kid he was all the rage. I had to learn dozens of his compositions.

Incidentally, the real drama of a concert comes when an artist both plays as soloist and conducts the orchestra. Dimitri Mitropoulos, a conductor who had always been consistently underrated despite the general acknowledgment of his talents, was one of the few people who could both play and conduct the Prokofiev Third. Bruno Walter's favorite for the same exhibition of virtuosity used to be the Mozart D Minor, and with Leonard Bernstein it is the Ravel Concerto.

When Mitropoulos was guest conductor at the New York Philharmonic, he wanted desperately to be appointed permanently to the post. He canvassed and lobbied as hard as he could. His efforts were in vain. Artur Rodzinsky was chosen. But Mitropoulos could always go back to his original post, that of conductor of the Minneapolis Symphony. The Minneapolis aggregation was not notorious for its high budgets, and this naturally limited the scope and number of players. So it was when I met Mitropoulos at the old Lotus Club on Fifty-seventh Street, just after he had failed in his coup directed toward the Philharmonic, that he heaved a sigh.

"Just think," he said lugubriously, "I shall probably never be able to use eight horns again."

Mitropoulos was always a practical person. One day we were watching Arturo Toscanini rehearse (a good many conductors and artists of this period were named Arthur, an international name, just as most English directors these days are named Peter). Mitropoulos listened to the maestro bawl out a clarinetist with all the fiery phrasing and gestures that Toscanini was capable of. Midway through the harangue, Mitropoulos turned to me and whispered: "Why doesn't he just tell him what he wants instead of shouting at him?"

"It would ruin the dramatic effect," I whispered back.

The manager of the New York Philharmonic, Bruno Zirato, the big likable Italian, made a rather refreshing observation about conductors. "People get tired of seeing only their backs," he confided. Bruno had also been associated with Toscanini, and before that he was secretary to the great Italian tenor, Enrico Caruso.

One of my letters from Laurence Stallings contains a description of his early memories of Caruso. I think it bears quoting:

> Caruso smoked backstage incessantly. I last saw him smoking before curtain time at Aida. They had a fireman following him to stamp out the butts, which he threw just anywhere. I was a Nubian slave in a black union-suit, carrying a ten-foot fly-swatter made of peacock feathers, and received $1 a night for keeping the flies off Mme. Louise Homer. . . . Caruso was a bundle of nerves; for he had to run that opening kickoff back 100 yards. Compared to Caruso, waiting to sing Celeste Aida without any warm-up, you, old boy, are as phlegmatic as a donkey. . . . Caruso also carried, in his brass belly-band, a small glass vial of gargle; and, as he approached Aida's throne, he snatched the vial out in clasped hands, made a gesture as if to say "My God, what loveliness," and turned his back to the audience, swallowed a sip of the stuff, or rather gargled it, then spit it all over me, and turned to his tormentor, Toscanini, and began the aria.

I must say that anyone with any kind of a mental process in his head beyond that of the aardvark finds it hard to spend his life in performing on the concert stage. It is not only the same uniform of white tie and tails, the same inadequate instruments, the same unperceptive audiences—but it is the all-embracing boredom of the act.

What is destructive to the artistic personality is to discover that the whole of the United States appears to be stamped out of the same die. All American towns have the same main street, the same stores, the same supermarkets, the same scenery and conversation, even the same Gideon Bibles in the same hotel rooms. The atmosphere is everywhere the same. The citizens appear to be duplicated from town to town.

On his concert tours, Jascha Heifetz was always bombarded with more invitations to dinners than he could possibly accept. Once in a while he would be intrigued by the news that a Jewish lady in a community enjoyed an enviable reputation as a Yiddish cook par excellence. He would then accept her dinner invitation with great expectations of gustatory delights.

Inevitably the hostess would be so overcome by the honor of having Heifetz in her home that she would rule out her customary Jewish cuisine as not being suitable for such an exalted occasion. Instead, she would serve her idea of an elegant meal— a half a grapefruit with a cherry on it and roast beef—exactly what Heifetz had been hoping to avoid.

Jascha Heifetz attended a vaudeville show—in the days when it was still popular—and there was a marvelous acrobatic turn performing. The man on stage played the violin in all sorts of poses, above his head, between his legs, across his back, while turning somersaults or standing on his head. Halfway through this display of incredible acrobatics, Heifetz turned to his companion with a frown. "Why doesn't he play it straight?" he asked.

I can still reminisce with anguish about my early concert days on the road. The pure physical effort involved over a period of time is frightful. Once I played in Atlanta, Georgia, then had to drive three hundred miles or so to Augusta. I got there after eight hours on the road. My hands were curled so tightly from nervous tension that I could hardly detach them from the wheel of the car, let alone play a concert.

In New Orleans, on the other hand, I was almost hit by an unwary driver while crossing the street. I so disliked being there that I not only accepted the man's apology but surprised him by saying: "With a little more skill, you could have hit me."

The famous New Orleans chicory coffee made me sick, and my piano was always out of tune. This is no reflection on the art of the piano tuner but simply the fact of climate. Artur Rubinstein has told me that, in his opinion, the two worst cities in the world for playing are Venice and New Orleans. Since they are either at or below sea level, the air is always moist. This not only makes pianos hard to tune; it is nearly impossible to depress the keys during a concert. To me, it felt like playing under water.

For years Artur Rubinstein, who is now in his late seventies, was the greatest nonsuccess in the country. His patience was, or should be, a legend all by itself, his art of waiting for his contemporaries to disappear. As time went by he became greater and greater; I shall always be grateful to him. During the years when he hadn't made the top rung as yet, he spent a great deal of time trying to cheer me up. Success always brought with it, for me, a deep depression, a weight of superguilt. I had my first real complex about being a public figure. Rubinstein and I inhabited the same New York delicatessen on Seventh Avenue. He was always brisk and cheerful, with a supply of sprightly stories, and he could give imitations, wonderful ones, of the dour Rachmaninoff and of people we both knew.

He is always amusing and his spirit perennially youthful. Occasionally his fellow artists resented his bounce. When he was in his fifties, Artur ran into the pianist Josef Hofmann in the Steinway Cellar—that gigantic room where the musicians select and test their instruments—and his spirits were irrepressible.

"Artur," Josef said gravely, "remember that you're not a boy wonder any more."

One of the terrible tragedies of music was the disintegration of Josef Hofmann as an artist. In his latter days he became an alcoholic. At his last public concert, which was a horrible ordeal for all of us, I asked Paul Bowles, who was then the assistant music critic of the New York *Herald Tribune,* to be kind in his review. It was gratifying to read that he was.

But Hofmann, whose glacial coolness was superior to that of any other artist on the platform, left a wonderful legacy. He was an elegant performer at the keyboard, a keyboard made especially for him because his hands were so small. When you realize how the full effect of the most difficult piano pieces depends almost entirely on the virtuosity of the player, you can realize what Hofmann did. There is a Chopin nocturne, for example, that is full of remarkably difficult trills. I have never heard anyone dare perform it in public except Hofmann. He did it impeccably—a major feat of musicianship. He possessed an ultrasensitive ear and an incredible memory. Rosina Lhévinne told me of one feat by Hofmann. He once heard her husband play a reasonably difficult and rather long composition, *The Lark,* by a Russian composer. Hofmann asked to hear it again—then sat down himself and played it absolutely correctly, note for note.

The finest visual compliment I ever witnessed came from a musician named Felix Salmond. It was given to Hofmann. Salmond heard a concert of the latter and went backstage to see him. There, the six foot six Salmond bent over the five foot five Hofmann and solemnly said: "You are a giant."

During my tours of popular *cum* classic music, I was one of the first pianists to play on a percentage take of the house. My road manager was Larry Fitzgerald, an eagle at the box office, whose own experience went back as a member of the entourage of Ignace Paderewski, after he was deposed as premier of Poland. By that time Paderewski was well on in years, but as a young man he had saved up his money to buy a new pair of shoes and finance a trip to Paris in order to hear the great Russian pianist, Anton Rubinstein (no relation to Artur). Unfortunately for Paderewski, the five recitals were sold out, and Rubinstein's manager, a man named Wolff, refused to find some way to accommodate the young pianist. Because of this deep disappointment Paderewski, during his own fame, always made certain that young students were able to attend his concerts. (As a young piano student I had the honor of playing one of his own compositions for him when he came to America.)

Another unfortunate incident of Paderewski's youth occurred at his debut in Berlin (he made his big impression in Paris). Hans von Bülow, the conductor, could not control his disinterest and actually yawned in full view of the audience as Paderewski was playing an encore. Paderewski never played Germany again.

Although Paderewski became the most famous figure in music and was received by all the crowned heads of Europe, he was never regarded too highly by many of his musical contemporaries. As a patriot interested in securing his country's freedom, he was made premier of Poland after World War I, largely due to the influence of President Wilson and Lord Balfour during the peace treaty at Versailles.

His tenure in office lasted for several years notwithstanding the fact that he was unaccustomed to the political machinations of his office, where he still kept concert-playing hours, sleeping until three in the afternoon. He was ultimately ousted by the strong man Pilsudski with the condition that he never return again to Poland.

When the grand old man toured this country in his private railroad car, complete with retinue and upright piano, he was the biggest concert draw ever seen up to that time—he actually filled Madison Square Garden with more than 20,000 people.

But in later years, when he was scheduled to play the Garden for the second time, he had become senile and his memory failed him. Although the house was sold out, he refused to appear. He said, "I have already played the concert," and insisted upon it. His managers could not convince him otherwise, so there was no alternative but to cancel the concert and refund the money.

Paderewski's last public appearance was on an NBC radio program in which he played his famous, but by then faded, *Minuet*—in his confusion he played it twice. He never regained his former virtuosity, and his decline was gradual. When he died forgotten at the Buckingham Hotel on Fifty-seventh Street in New York City, it was a tragic end for a figure who at the height of his musical fame was unchallengeable.

In Russia it was Anton Rubinstein who had made the role of a musician acceptable in terms of a profession—never before had it been allowed to appear on a passport.

Anton Rubinstein, helped in his career by the Grand Duchess Helena and a favorite at the court, founded two famous conservatories, the Moscow and the St. Petersburg. One of the greatest pianists of all time, he wanted most of all to be a composer, but was surpassed in this by his most illustrious pupil, Tchaikovsky. During his lifetime Rubinstein's music was accepted with acclaim, although it has slowly and completely disappeared from the contemporary scene.

An anecdote concerning Anton Rubinstein was told to me by the writer Lesley Blanch, who is an authority on Russian history. She said that when Anton Rubinstein was touring Russia he arrived in a small town and was greeted by the mayor. The mayor told him that the postman was an amateur cellist and that it was the greatest desire of his life to play once with the famous pianist. Rubinstein genially agreed to play with him. They went to his home. The postman tremblingly unsheathed his cello and sat down. He drew his bow across the strings for the first note and collapsed.

"He was so overcome," said Miss Blanch, "that he died of a heart attack."

My reaction to her story was terrible. I had a pain in my heart for weeks afterward.

A young musical student who had heard Anton Rubinstein play and who had been deeply and everlastingly impressed was Sergei Rachmaninoff.

Rachmaninoff, it is interesting to note, had a nervous breakdown after the performance of his first symphony. He underwent two years of intensive therapy, probably the first such program in musical history. This I can understand. They even brought in Tolstoi to cheer him up. This I cannot understand.

I was present at Rachmaninoff's last New York recital at Carnegie Hall, and if my memory is correct, the program consisted of the Chopin Polonaise in C Minor and the Nocturne in F Sharp Major, the first part of Schumann's last *Novellette*, Beethoven's Sonata Opus III, the Liszt transcriptions of several of Schubert's lieder, and among the encores, a transcription of his own song "Daisy."

(Which reminds me of Artur Rubinstein's comment on some of Rachmaninoff's compositions for the piano: "You have to have six fingers on each hand to play them.")

To my knowledge, Rachmaninoff never played Debussy or Ravel, and the only piano concerto that he played, outside of his own compositions, was the Beethoven No. 1. With one exception. Rachmaninoff decided to play the Schumann piano concerto for the first time late in his career with the Pittsburgh Symphony. Bakaleinikov, the conductor, revered Rachmaninoff as did most Russians. The Schumann piece starts with one note played by the orchestra—the soloist responds by playing a cascade of chords for two bars. At the rehearsal Rachmaninoff smudged the opening so much that Bakaleinikov stopped short. In order to spare the great artist any embarrassment he proceeded to excoriate the entire orchestra for a bad job on that one note. Rachmaninoff knew what he meant; he played the concert, but it was hell for him and he never played it again.

Oddly enough, Brahms himself had a difficult time playing the same concerto.

I also recall what Diaghilev, the Russian ballet impresario, said. His theory was that the playing of Schumann's music was of such a personal nature that it should be strictly a private affair between the pianist and the piano—with no audience allowed.

In 1940 I first played with Pierre Monteux, the genial lion who created the San Francisco Symphony virtually out of thin air. He told me he had just been to Belgium and that the famed piano virtuoso Moritz Rosenthal, at the age of seventy-five, had again after forty years played Chopin's Concerto No. 1 in E Minor. He amused Monteux after the concert by declaring: "Now I think I'll learn the Chopin Concerto Number Two." This was a joke about his small repertory.

Moritz Rosenthal had a considerable reputation for wit. When pianist Artur Schnabel was turned down by the draft for World War I because he couldn't pass the physical, Rosenthal's comment was: "No fingers."

This leads to another Rosenthal remark. Eugène d'Albert was a great keyboard technician. He wrote an opera called *Tiefland*. Although it originally had a limited success, it is now in limbo. Perhaps this came about for the same reason that Moritz Rosenthal supplied. Upon seeing D'Albert's enormous musical library, the numerous scores and compositions of various composers, Rosenthal quipped, "I thought you composed out of inspiration—not out of memory."

One of D'Albert's wives, Teresa Carenño, was also famous as a pianist, which did not particularly please him. He married six times. The late William Steinway was credited with the remark that if D'Albert married again he could be billed as the Bluebeard of the Piano.

Moritz Rosenthal in his youth had been a pupil of Franz Liszt. It was a master class, and some of the less talented pupils drove Liszt crazy playing Chopin's Minute Waltz over and over again. Liszt, in desperation, finally had Rosenthal transcribe and play this hackneyed composition in thirds and sixths, quite a prodigious technical feat. The idea was to dissuade the pupils from playing it.

The later piano works of Liszt were harmonically so inventive and new that they were the forerunner of the Impressionist school that Debussy founded.

Liszt was also very fond of female companionship, if not of wives. It is a fact that he went to Rome, took the orders, and became an abbé—despite the fact that he had fathered three illegitimate children. This shows, I think, how liberal the Papacy can be when it tries.

The women in his life paid Liszt back for his attitude. His second mistress smoked cigars and wrote twenty-four volumes on some obscure aspect of Catholicism.

Liszt, of course, is one of the patron saints of the piano. Horowitz, who is extraordinarily free of other superstitions, carries a picture of Liszt inside his coat to every concert.

The small repertoire of Moritz Rosenthal recalls the story about when musicians were asked to sign a special fan for a woman patron. A pianist—Vladimir de Pachmann by name—came up for his turn and someone said mischievously: "There's room on the handle for your complete repertoire."

De Pachmann had a habit, when playing difficult passages, of covering one hand with the other, so that other pianists would not be able to copy his special fingering.

I cherish the tale about a certain pianist named Ferruccio Busoni. He loved Chopin's works. He insisted on playing them in public, in spite of the fact that he was an atrocious interpreter. At one of his concerts, one of the pupils of Chopin, a Polish count, leaped up in the front row after one particularly painful rendition. He cried: "In the name of Frédéric Chopin, I protest!"

When Busoni was scheduled to play Beethoven's Emperor Concerto in Vienna, conductor Gustav Mahler was so anxious about the performance that he met Busoni at the station and hummed the right tempo all the way to the rehearsal hall.

After another performance of the same concerto in Boston, Busoni announced with satisfaction that he had not used the pedal at all. I never heard of anyone doing that before, or since as a matter of fact. The pedal is not only very important to the music—it can cover up a lot of mistakes.

An example of one incident, based on the wandering qualities of the mind, could be illustrated by what happened to Jacques Thibaud. Playing as violin soloist on tour in Europe, without a rehearsal, Thibaud somehow convinced himself on one particular occasion that he was playing the Beethoven Violin Concerto. In that piece, the orchestra plays for approximately two minutes before the soloist starts to play. In truth, Thibaud was actually playing a Mendelssohn composition—which gives the soloist roughly one and a half bars before his entrance. Thibaud came out of his reverie at the last second, but he really had to rip into it.

Which is reminiscent of the time that an interviewer asked me what happened when I took Demerol before a concert. "Well," I said with all deliberate speed, "I begin the first movement rather slowly."

I wonder how many people remember that John Erskine, the critic-author-teacher, used to sit down with an orchestra and play the McDowell piano concerto. As a young man, Erskine had studied music at Columbia University with the prominent American composer Edward McDowell.

Along with his professorship at Columbia, Erskine headed the Juilliard Institute of Music and wrote several books including a bestseller, *Helen of Troy*. At a Town Hall forum debate on music, Erskine had as his opponent the young composer William Schuman. Schuman's knowledge of modern music was so superior to that of Erskine, he not only beat him in the debate, he replaced him at Juilliard. Schuman went from there to head the Schirmer music publishing house, and now serves in the same capacity at the world-renowned New York Lincoln Center.

The living dean of contemporary composers is without a doubt Igor Stravinsky. In the middle fifties, Stravinsky was commissioned by the Venice Festival to write them an original work. His contribution turned out to be fifteen minutes long. The officials of the festival complained to Stravinsky that this was too short.

"Well, then," Stravinsky replied calmly, "play it again."

Since that time, Virgil Thomson has christened him "the merchant of Venice."

But the rewards of composers are not always calculable. Stravinsky, for example, suffered from this. For years he received no royalties from *The Firebird* or *Petrouchka* or even *Le Sacre du Printemps,* because they were published in Russia where international copyright laws are not recognized. Then, in the 1940's, he reorchestrated and revised all these compositions. This brought them under copyright laws of the United States, and he began to get what he deserved in remuneration.

In my opinion Stravinsky's books and magazine articles, in conjunction with Robert Craft, contain some of the most ironic, savage, and saturnine wit of our time. I think the osmosis of Stravinsky's adopting Schoenberg's serial system was due to Robert Craft—quite a brilliant Renaissance man and a former Schoenberg pupil. Originally the two famous composers loathed each other, yet Stravinsky's written pieces now show reluctant affection and respect for Schoenberg. Actually, Stravinsky admires very few musical people, with the exception of the French conductor-composer Pierre Boulez, whom he rebukes occasionally for his fast tempi, and Karl Czerny (1791-1857), the Austrian composer, who wrote finger exercises for the piano, with perfect structure. Stravinsky became acquainted with Czerny's work back in 1925 when he was to appear as piano soloist in his own neoclassic concerto. In order to improve his technique, he practiced Czerny exercises. As far back as 1913, when Stravinsky played his *Sacre du Printemps* on the piano in a private performance for the first time, he revealed music that was to cause a riot at its first public performance; music so rhythmically and harmonically dissonant, so cacaphonous and relentless, that Diaghilev, who was present, asked in astonishment: "How long will this go on?"

Without missing a note Stravinsky replied, "Forever, my dear."

Although Stravinsky wrote only one major opera, *The Rake's Progress,* with libretto by W. H. Auden, it had been rumored years back that he contemplated doing an opera with Dylan Thomas. It is a pity it never came off; it would have been an unusual work that combined two such disparate personalities.

In the forties the late Billy Rose produced a Broadway show, *The Seven Lively Arts,* for which Stravinsky wrote a ballet. After the opening Billy sent a telegram to Stravinsky: "Ballet great success. Would be greater if you reorchestrate it."

Stravinsky wired back: "Content with great success."

An unflattering piece about Stravinsky was written for a magazine sometime ago by the composer-songwriter Vernon Duke. (When he writes serious music he uses his real name, Vladimir Dukelsky.)

Stravinsky's angry reply was in the form of an article for the same magazine. His opening line was: *Obliterate V.D.!*—and that was only the beginning; he dredged up Vernon's musical failures, made fun of his successes, and referred to him only by his initials.

It was obvious that Stravinsky will brook no criticism.

I watched him on television last year when he was photographed at the University of Texas. A student asked for his opinion of the composer Richard Strauss. With his charming lethal smile, the impish octogenarian stated that he disliked all of Strauss' works, major and minor, and that included *Der Rosenkavalier*.

When I had recovered from my astonishment I said to my wife: "Well, he has the right to be jealous—*Rosenkavalier* is the most successful opera in the twentieth century."

According to his wife, Vera, Stravinsky has always had a hypochondriacal preoccupation with medicine of all kinds. And like most Europeans an abiding interest in liquor.

When Stravinsky consulted with Dr. Niehans of Switzerland, famed for his rejuvenating treatments to prominent members of the geriatric set, he was informed that one of the requisites to becoming a patient was the total abstinence from alcoholic beverages.

"Good-bye, Doctor," was his reply, as he hastily took his departure.

I recall the time at Chasen's restaurant in Hollywood when the great composer came over to my booth. He grabbed my hand and said: "Malady?"

"Oh," I said, "I haven't composed in twenty years."

He shook his head and said again: "Malady?"

"No," I said warmly and distinctly. "I haven't put a note on paper."

Stravinsky drew back and said impatiently: "Sick, sick, sick!" He had actually been inquiring about my health.

Chapter 7

*W*HEN I met Truman Capote at a dinner in Beverly Hills, *In Cold Blood* had been written but had not yet been published. He was accompanied by three of his friends from the Garden City murder case—the police captain, the captain's wife, and the widow of the Kansas judge. Truman, one of the pets of the international set (according to a detractor, he works hard to be loved), has access to all the great houses; consequently, he and his friends were invited everywhere.

At one dinner party we were informed that a prominent social figure had given him twenty gift treatments from a well-known beauty doctor at a hundred bucks a throw. I asked him why. Capote pointed to a spot just under his left nostril and said: "I've got a mark here."

171

I looked closely and said: "I can't see anything at all."

"You have to have a very strong light," Capote said complacently.

That was the night I sat next to the widow of the judge who chattered on and on, nervously and interminably. As I left after that exhausting evening, I said to Capote: "Five more minutes and you'd have had another murder to write about!"

I am indebted to Capote for some additions and improvements to my library of superstitions, phobias, and psychoses. I have a whole collection that relates to hotels (especially in Philadelphia), and Truman told me that he has slept in lobbies many times because of his own misgivings.

Truman, along with other authors, has made records of his own stories. He also narrated for television his deeply touching and beautiful work "A Christmas Memory." When he did the talking record of *In Cold Blood,* however, a critic opined that the author's speaking voice proved more of a disservice than a help. There is a slight touch of "the bald soprano" about Truman's vocal projection.

The latest heavyweight literary brawl has taken place between Truman Capote and Kenneth Tynan. Because of Tynan's association with the National Theatre, he cannot ethically write drama criticism. But that doesn't stop him from writing on other subjects. His review of *In Cold Blood* for the London *Observer* caused a sensation. It was a devastating personal attack on Capote, that questioned, accused, and denounced him and the motives involved in writing about the Kansas murder case. Jonathan Miller summed it up when he said: "Truman got what the criminals were after."

In the following issue, Truman blasted back in a fulminating rage. Phrases like "the guts of a butterfly" were wildly hurled about, and the angry exchange of name-calling, foot-stomping articles went on for weeks. My.

One day in Sardi's restaurant in New York, a woman at the

next table turned to me and said: "I'm Mrs. Kenneth Tynan."
I recalled her vaguely. We had met ten years before. She was
the former (now again) Elaine Dundy. She told me she had
just finished a new novel about an aging critic, *The Old Man
and Me*.

"You must have had Cyril Connolly in mind," I said. She
thought I was psychic. During World War II, Connolly, a distinguished English literary critic, edited *Horizon*—the best
magazine I read in that ten-year period. His books *Ideas and
Places* and *The Condemned Playground* bear rereading.

I have always found Elaine very entertaining—as a person
as well as a novelist. I incline to agree with what she told me
about Enid Bagnold, the English writer and author of *Serena
Blandish* and *National Velvet*. The elderly lady is now in her
eighties and takes two Dexedrine tablets every morning to pep
herself up for the day. "What," she asked Elaine, "did writers
do before they invented Dexedrine?" I know part of the answer: at the Mermaid Tavern, they used canary wine.

Elaine joined the camp followers of psychiatry. She told me
she had the same psychoanalyst as Tennessee Williams and was
right after his confessional on the couch. "That must be a hard
act to follow," I said.

One of the psychiatrists who treated me at various times had
at one point been on the staff of St. Elizabeth's in Washington,
the hospital which had sheltered Ezra Pound, the poet. He told
me that while he was there, Pound won the Bollingen Prize for
poetry. It was a cash award of a thousand dollars. All the patients became very excited; they thought Pound would use part
of the money to buy them a television set. Pound refused. My
own opinion is that Pound is a great poet, all right, but not a
great man if you happen to be a Jew.

When the police put on a drive to put down prostitution in

London, it was the novelist Nancy Mitford who said the enchanting line: "But where will our young men learn?"

In the same way, I got involved in a discussion about young Prince Charles of England. We were worrying about how the youngster would get his sex education. "Don't worry," I told them, "Prince Philip will take care of it."

The two great writers who have never let me down over the years are Samuel Johnson and Oscar Wilde. They always manage to brighten my life with something new, full of flavor, and to the point. Johnson's familiar line, "Patriotism is the last refuge of a scoundrel," came to mind recently when I read a review of John Osborne's play *Inadmissible Evidence*. The critic Elizabeth Hardwicke paraphrased Johnson when she wrote in defense of the Osborne work, "A well-made play is the last refuge of a hack."

One of the outstanding marriages of modern literature was that of Jean Stafford, the novelist, and Robert Lowell, the Pulitzer Prize poet. I think it marked the greatest literary juncture since the Brownings. After their divorce they were again married to writers—she to the late Joe Liebling of the *New Yorker* magazine, Lowell to Elizabeth Hardwicke, an editor of the *New York Review*.

Besides the esteem that Lowell enjoys in this country, he has also begun to receive acclaim from England's literary critics.

My friend Goddard Lieberson, president of Columbia Records, introduced me to Robert Lowell the night of the day his "Benito Cereno" was recorded.

We all had dinner in the Oak Room at the New York Plaza Hotel. Lowell was slightly sloshed and garrulous, but he looks the way a poet should look. As a matter of fact, I told him that he reminded me of a Gentile Clifford Odets. The scholarly appearance was what I meant.

"I've been committed to twelve sanitariums," he announced with an air of triumph. "How about you?"

Who counts? "Ten," I said at random. I didn't want a contest. But I remembered that it was Robert Frost who had called Lowell for his expert advice when his son became mentally ill.

At the dinner we hit on other subjects. The name of Lincoln Kirstein, financial backer of the American Ballet Company, came into the conversation. "Kirstein is the King David of the ballet," I volunteered.

Lowell turned his attention to June. "What do you think of Stonewall Jackson?" he asked for openers. He engaged her in conversation and learned that she was half Irish. "But do you *feel* Irish?" he inquired. June told how her father used to sing songs like "Who Put the Overalls in Mrs. Clancy's Chowder?" and "The Wearing of the Green." Lowell, intrigued, asked her to sing the last one, so June obliged. In the Oak Room at the Plaza Hotel!

My wife can sing about four bars on key. After that, the song sounds like an Arnold Schoenberg composition.

In the meantime, I had been excluded from all of this jollity. When the poet said good night to us, he observed penitently: "I've been very rude to you, Oscar."

"I've noticed it," I said.

One of my doctors used to be on the staff of the Camarillo State Hospital. In California, that hospital is one of those which caters to the foibles of the mentally ill. He told me that a great many killers who execute the most terrible crimes really have no conscience. In my case it is different. I have a hyperactive conscience and no crime.

That is a morbid subject. Speaking of the word, I recently had a distinguished visitor, Eric Ambler, the English writer of novels about murder and espionage. He told me he had once visited a sanitarium devoted to therapy for practically incurable criminals. One of the patients was a murderer who explained patiently to Ambler that he had been framed. He had not plunged the sword into the man's skull. He had merely been withdrawing the sword when someone came in.

"He *was* crazy," Eric said authoritatively. "You don't plunge a sword into a man's skull. You look for a soft spot."

Each time I see Eric I am given a full treatise on his opinions. He told me that his mother and father were music hall performers. "They gradually moved up to a better class," Ambler said. In 1922 his father suddenly bought a motor car. It made Ambler furious at the time. The reason for his rage was that his father spent the money which had been put aside for his tuition in school. It still makes him turn purple.

I cannot say that I blame him. He had worked hard for a good education. He was one of four, picked out of hundreds, who won a scholarship to a university—and he got 100 in a chemistry test, which I consider marvelous. As it was, he spent sixteen years in a state of poverty before he succeeded. He even did a vaudeville turn and still can play the piano.

Ambler has had a productive writing career, with eighteen novels to his credit. Yet there was a period of ten years in his life—six years spent in the British army, the rest in the film industry—when he almost lost his ability to write in novel form. It was Noel Coward, according to Eric, who talked him into resuming book writing. "You think you will always be able to go back to the well," Noel admonished him. "That may be so but remember this; if you stay away too long, one day you will go back and find the well dry!"

Ambler went back to the well and has been turning out successful novels ever since.

The observation by Kenneth Tynan that George Bernard Shaw's plays do not inspire affection disturbed me, so I approached Ambler for his opinion. He more or less agreed with

Tynan with the exception of *Heartbreak House*. Ambler's comment about *Candida,* the G.B.S. play about marriage, bears repeating. "That play," said Eric, "is Shaw's *Who's Afraid of Virginia Woolf!*"

In a general discussion of writers, Eric remarked that when you see a picture like *Alfie,* you know damn well that it could not have been written by a homosexual. And as for American mystery writers, he prefers Raymond Chandler, for instance, to Dashiell Hammett.

The late Dashiell Hammett, a tall, thin, handsome man, was a former Pinkerton detective. The Pinkerton detective agency, dating back to 1850, was notable among other things for thwarting a plot against the life of Abraham Lincoln. The abortive assassination attempt was to have taken place in Baltimore when the President-elect arrived there on his historical journey from Springfield, Illinois, to Washington.

Allan Pinkerton, the founder of the agency, was also responsible for developing our present Federal secret service department.

At one time, Dash Hammett had been assigned by the Pinkerton agency to uncover a gold cache illegally headed for Australia. In a display of ingenuity, he discovered the treasure before the ship even sailed, thereby canceling himself out of the trip that he had been anticipating.

Hammett, who served in both World Wars, was the first to ask, "How to tell a fairy from an Englishman." (It sounded like a good song title.) His private name for successful music composers was "peacocks," which I thought a good description. (They usually preen themselves and are filled with self-esteem.)

It was generally believed among their friends that Dash was a mentor in the career of his close friend Lillian Hellman. Whether or not that was so, Hammett himself wrote very little after the production of Lillian's first play, *The Children's Hour.* Dash had his turn as a Hollywood "wonder boy" when his

Thin Man stories became popular movies. His book *The Maltese Falcon* served as the directorial debut for writer John Huston, whose brilliant screenplay *Sergeant York* won him great acclaim.

The celebrated Gertrude Stein, a detective story buff, was especially fond of Hammett's novels. He was the one person she personally expressed a desire to meet when she visited Hollywood in the thirties. She wrote about their meeting in her book *Everybody's Autobiography* and, incidentally, misspelled his last name. Or else her proofreader decided that a rose is a rose is a rose by any other name.

A year or so ago Lillian Hellman wrote an article about Hammett in which she disclosed that the witty dialogue between Nick Charles and his wife Nora in the *Thin Man* stories was based on their own personal exchanges.

The Hellman plays were so powerful and created such a forcible impact that George S. Kaufman's reaction was, "You know you've been in a fight!" A lawyer's opinion was given by Morris Ernst, when he observed that the Hellman plays are based on blackmail. When you consider *The Little Foxes, Another Part of the Forest,* and *Toys in the Attic,* you can appreciate his analysis.

The Little Foxes had its successful run in the pre-World War II period. When Russia attacked Finland, Broadway shows rushed to the aid of "poor little Finland" by giving benefit performances.

Lillian Hellman refused to follow suit, precipitating an intense feud with the star Tallulah Bankhead, who never forgave her.

Another Part of the Forest, the second Hellman play about the avaricious Hubbard family, was the Broadway debut of Patricia Neal in the part of the young Regina. Years later when I met her, she said that it hadn't been good luck starting her career with so prominent a role.

Lillian Hellman also did the libretto for an unsuccessful opera based on Voltaire's *Candide*. The music was supplied by Leonard Bernstein, who used to climb up on Lillian's lap at parties. Lenny never overlooked the opportunity to appeal to the maternal instincts.

When I was young, Dashiell Hammett was the first one who told me (and quite enthusiastically) about the sardonic author Ambrose Bierce. And Lillian Hellman was good enough to recommend other authors for me to read. One of them was Stendhal, the *nom de plume* for Marie Henri Beyle.

One of my rarest books is an 1818 biography of three composers: *Vies de Haydn, de Mozart, de Métastase*. It was written by L. A. C. Bombet, another name for Stendhal, who also used various pseudonyms in his personal life.

Booth Tarkington was a boyhood favorite of mine. Today he is out of fashion, but in his time he won two Pulitzer Prizes hands down. I was startled on my 1959 television show when author Leon Uris appeared and said with a great deal of self-assurance, "That man from Indiana had better watch himself." I went back to my childhood. I thought he was comparing himself to Tarkington, who had written a novel, *The Gentleman from Indiana*. It was a relief to find out that he only meant James Jones, who came from *Illinois*.

In my youth, I read all the good Russian authors such as Feodor Dostoevski, Leo Tolstoi, Anton Chekhov, and Ivan Turgenev. Youth is the period when they should be read. After I passed that age in life, I was never able to stand their morbid attitude about existence. With the exception of an occasional Chekhov play, I never looked at them again.

The depth of Dostoevski's characterizations and the complexity of his protagonists made other writers, Dickens for example, appear pallid by comparison. Tolstoi is, by all accounts, the author's author. Though he lived to as late as 1910, he never won the Nobel Prize. And that is a terrible thing to say about the Nobel Prize.

Another enthusiasm of mine—and a personal revelation—were the books with one-word titles (*Loving, Nothing,* etc.) of Henry Green, the pseudonym of the Birmingham businessman-author. I read them in 1952 when I was convalescing from my heart attack and found them brilliantly amusing. The last time I saw Elaine Dundy, she mentioned that when she lived in England she arranged a meeting between Green and the satirical author Terry Southern, who was also his great admirer. That was before Southern wrote *Candy.*

To demonstrate how engrossed I was simply in the act of reading, I once plowed through a 700-page-plus biography of Lord Horatio Nelson, the English naval hero, merely because I had heard that his last words were "Kiss me, Hardy." Hardy happened to be the second mate of Nelson's flagship when the admiral got it. There was nothing particularly significant in two males kissing each other, but it was a wonderful last line. After that, I heard a theory that Nelson could have said, "Kismet, Hardy"—the Turkish word meaning "destiny."

I believe the original story.

Once I was driven to read the memoirs of Thomas Carlyle. I struggled through nearly 150 pages of his description of every breath of his dying father. Afterward I learned that Virginia Woolf in her diary (expunged by her husband, the publisher Leonard Woolf) described it as a "grave-digger's lament." I never agreed more heartily with any opinion.

Incidentally, Leonard Woolf's autobiography revealed that the diagnosis of Virginia Woolf as a schizophrenic was made on the second day of their marriage.

Nowadays, it is strange to think that, aside from H. L. Mencken and his occasional plugs, there were few literary cults of the twenties, and only a handful of little magazines where they cooked up feuds to promote their own personal success.

Ernest Hemingway was hardly known. I think the first critic to mention him seriously was Burton Rascoe.

I met Hemingway once, and the man breathed so heavily he frightened me.

Hemingway always sought to prove that he was a he-man and felt that his hairy chest—like an exploded mattress—proved it. This brought about a classic encounter between him and John Huston. When he met Huston they were both a little under the weather. Hemingway told Huston: "If it weren't for the movies, you wouldn't be considered a writer."

Well, naturally, after that one word led to another, and Hemingway challenged the other to a boxing match with gloves. Hemingway cocked his fist and Huston conveniently fell down. Afterward, John pointed out that he was so drunk that he could not stand up. Huston claimed to be an amateur boxing champion, but at a Hollywood party when he tangled with Errol Flynn, he was knocked down twenty times in succession.

When Clifton Fadiman and I met recently, I noted that there have been three self-styled "champs" in our time—Hemingway, Picasso, and Stravinsky. Fadiman replied, "And the weakest of the three is Hemingway."

I must mention here that F. Scott Fitzgerald has been credited by certain people as helping Hemingway to write. For his part, Hemingway always insisted that it was the other way around. I don't intend to get embroiled in this except to recall an ironic line of Fitzgerald's: "Show me a hero and I'll write you a tragedy." Sadly enough it applies to both of them.

Speaking of Clifton Fadiman reminds me that his hobby is collecting information about the last moments of great authors. A rather morbid interest as far as I am concerned. "The day Proust finished his book," Fadiman said, "he wrote *finis* on the manuscript and the next day he died."

"It would have been nice if he could have read the reviews," I replied.

Fadiman made me even gloomier by telling me that when André Gide died the crowds jeered at his funeral—and that the same thing had happened to Anatole France.

After Fadiman read my *Memoirs of an Amnesiac* (and wrote a vastly entertaining piece about it for *Holiday* magazine), he called up my wife and told her that I reminded him of Jean Jacques Rousseau. Not as a writer, naturally, but in relation to my epidermis. It is Fadiman's contention that if I had another extra layer or so of skin I would have more protection against the vicissitudes of existence. (At least I *think* that's what he means.)

Anyway, in light of (or in spite of) his perceptive insight, it was his wife who called me after my *Memoirs* were published.

"Oscar," she said cheerfully, "you have two bad reviews and both of them are on front pages." I did not get over that information for a month. No elephant hide, I.

Robert Kirsch is the book editor of the Los Angeles *Times,* a fairly influential paper. When he favorably reviewed my *Memoirs* he wrote that there hasn't been a book comparable since Thomas De Quincey's *Confessions of an English Opium-Eater,* with the difference, he added, that mine was funny. "Most people are self-centered," he wrote, "but Oscar Levant is a city of one."

Well, naturally, after that I had to call him up. He came to my house and we discussed a mutual acquaintance.

As a patient in a psychiatric hospital, I had met another patient, a boy of college age, who said he was in a UCLA writing class taught by Robert Kirsch.

I asked Kirsch if he remembered him. "Of course," he said, "he was very bright."

"I was shocked to read that he had taken a shot at his parents," I added.

"Isn't that every boy's dream?" asked Kirsch.

Could be, could be.

Because of the publication of my *Memoirs,* which contained a description of the practices in Los Angeles mental hospitals, some changes have been made for the better. The doctor I praised in the book, who at first I personally disliked but who was an excellent man, has been made the head of one institution. Perhaps I overpraised him. But I did think he was very good at feeling my pulse.

As for critics, in my opinion no writer should ever give a lunch to the English critic Malcolm Muggeridge—for the writer's own protection. He had lunch with Somerset Maugham, Max Beerbohm, and Ian Fleming and then wrote devastating attacks against each one of them; worse, he complained about the food. The only two great men of the century that Muggeridge has really liked, as far as my researches go, have been Joseph Stalin—who killed 19,000,000 people—and Charles de Gaulle. When Muggeridge interviewed Brendan Behan on a BBC television show, I read that he plied him with liquor. As someone said, that was like pouring water over Niagara Falls.

All hell broke loose in England when Muggeridge directed one of his more scathing articles against the Queen herself. His antiestablishment policies are unusual for a man of his generation.

Needless to say, Muggeridge is an unparalleled writer, a master of humor as well as diatribe—idol-smashing is his "bag."

You can imagine how relieved I was to discover that his review of my book in *Esquire* magazine was both favorable and sympathetic.

"*The Memoirs of an Amnesiac,* then, may be regarded as a sort of casebook of our time," he wrote.

And about the author Muggeridge said: "He seems to me to be one of those truly unquenchable human beings in whom the flame of light burns very brightly, but who, just by virtue of that circumstance, finds its strains and tensions the more agonizing; sometimes unbearably so."

At the present time I am slightly quenchable.

Once Jack Paar had Malcolm Muggeridge on his television show. They had a long discussion of pornography in its more elevated aspects. As I was the next guest, Parr asked me what I thought about pornography. I confined myself to two words: "It helps."

As a guest at the home of James and Pamela Mason—when they happened to be married—I was assigned to a seat next to a lady who I was told was the wife of Romain Gary, author and French consul in Los Angeles. I was fresh out of the hospital, but grim and alert. As we talked, I said, "For the wife of a French consul, you speak very good English." She then pointed out, to my embarrassment, that she was a native Englishwoman, whose maiden name was Lesley Blanch—a fine novelist in her own right.

Her clipped British accent reminded me of what Moss Hart had said of the English: "They talk like that straight from the womb."

When the Garys lived in Hollywood in 1960, they were both engaged in writing books: he on *Promise at Dawn,* she on *Sabres of Paradise.* Mrs. Gary described the rigorous lives that married authors lead. Engrossed in their labors, she said, they scarcely saw each other for days at a time, encountering each other fleetingly in the hallway now and then, disheveled and exhausted.

Romain Gary, in the French tradition of author-diplomat, would have eventually attained an ambassadorship had he continued with his diplomatic career. Instead, he chose to give it up when his term ran out as the French consul in Los Angeles, and devote all of his time to writing. His marriage to Lesley

Blanch broke up, and when he remarried a few years later it was to the actress Jean Seberg.

Long before I had drugs, my real boosters were books. I thought it was I alone who discovered Ivy Compton-Burnett. I read about six books by this excellent English novelist and then talked loftily about her to Lesley Blanch, who at one time was also the editor of *Vogue* in London. She informed me that Ivy Compton-Burnett was indeed known by others and that she, in fact, had done a whole layout on her. Thereupon I lost interest in her as a discovery but continued my admiration. Her novels are written almost entirely in dialogue—so brilliant that it makes T. S. Eliot sound like Johnny Carson. Her pages present three- and four-year-old boys holding forth in conversations that would be the equivalent of those between Winston Churchill and George Bernard Shaw. *Sui generis,* she is only for the select, or rather the addicted, few.

As a writer, I consider Mary McCarthy a phenomenon's phenomenon. She is always willing to seek out another author's jugular vein. I was surprised, therefore, when I heard her say on a taped television interview from Paris that the prospect of interviewing the elderly Ivy Compton-Burnett filled her with awe.

Some of the other McCarthy remarks were interesting. She said, in effect, that a writer is spoiled by becoming a writer; he is almost always autobiographical in his first book, then the mechanics of writing forces him into an isolation that makes him an observer rather than a participant.

A metropolitan writer, Miss McCarthy finds it difficult not to see the grotesque side of life. She finds herself in the position of someone who, in the process of telling a story, gets halfway through and then discovers it is all terribly funny. This happens to her when she writes. It also happened to Stendhal, she said.

She noted that George Eliot, the only woman author to write

on universal themes, lived in the midlands. And Faulkner, she
said, could only have written the way he did, living in a community.

The novelist, she continued, can be disturbed that his subject matter, compared to world conditions, will seem inconse-
quential. But, she added, he must push this idea firmly aside
and get on with his writing.

I met Mary McCarthy once years ago, at Virgil Thomson's
Chelsea Hotel apartment. I can say for a fact that on that occasion we exchanged not a single word.

Apart from his musical knowledge—he actually hates music,
I think, but he writes about it brilliantly—Virgil Thomson is
a stimulating conversationalist. I relish his stories. On the occasion of one of our meetings he greeted me with the hackneyed
expression, "How are you, Oscar?"

"My health is a thing of national concern," I said pettishly.

Virgil regarded me gravely. "You make it so, dear Oscar,"
he said.

I also remember a remark of Virgil's after my *Memoirs* were
published. "You can always get a good book out of a bad habit,"
he said.

Virgil is an extraordinarily good sleeper. Possibly this is because he is very easily bored; but the sound of applause always
wakes him up. He can doze through the most cacaphonous
modern composition or even through the screening of a dirty
Jean Genet picture. The cycle of imported Italian pictures is,
in Virgil Thomson's words, "entirely occupied with mamas and
the priests."

One evening at a dinner with Virgil, Christopher Isherwood
plied him with questions about James Joyce. Christopher, an
English expatriate, was interested in learning how the great
Irish author felt about living in France. "It was not a problem,"
said Virgil, who had known Joyce in the early days. Virgil also
confided that he had been asked by Joyce to set a chapter of

Finnegan's Wake to music. His refusal was based on the fact that he was closely affiliated with Gertrude Stein and was in no position to be disloyal. (Which reminds me that as far back as 1918, Virginia Woolf in *The Common Reader* picked James Joyce as a great writer: quite an anticipation of the academic taste.)

The Thomson-Stein collaboration had begun in Paris in the late twenties. *Four Saints in Three Acts,* produced in New York in 1934, music by Thomson, libretto by Stein, was the first opera with an all-Negro cast. Their other work, *The Mother of Us All,* performed in 1947, after Gertrude Stein's death, was her last literary effort.

All of Gertrude Stein's charm—which for me is considerable—comes from simple words used with complex meanings. I concur in her remark (paraphrased): "If you haven't seen a friend in seventeen years, you might just as well forget it."

For years Virgil Thomson planned an opera based on the life of George Gordon Noel, Lord Byron. He explained to me why it should be a success, giving five very cogent reasons.

"First," he said, "Byron was a successful romantic poet. Second, he had a title. Third, he had a good deal of money. Fourth, he was lame. Fifth, he had two children, due to incest with his sister."

"With his half-sister," I replied learnedly.

"With his two half-sisters!" Virgil returned.

I personally think that Virgil wrote it because Byron was such a great satirist.

According to another source, the reason that Lady Byron left the poet's bed and board suddenly and inexplicably was because he tried to make a "rear entrance."

Only one thing disturbed Virgil about his Byronetta. He said that Byron's death by fever in Greece was undramatic. I advised him to read again the last scenes in *Fathers and Sons* by Turgenev.

We were also talking about the cyclical renaissance of academic interest in various authors. I settled on Edith Wharton.

"She was the first woman of high society in New York to become an author of distinction," I said, forgetting Harriet Beecher Stowe for the moment. "It was very unusual because New York society frowned on writing."

"The hell with Edith Wharton," Virgil said. "I'm a Gertrude Stein man myself."

"Well," I told him, "the only author from New York that I feel sympathetic with these days is Washington Irving."

"I have come to the conclusion," Virgil said, "that Irving was a homosexual."

The chores of writing have other problems. Once I asked Virgil why another music critic, Arthur Berger, quit criticizing (a position of power) and took a teaching post at Brandeis University. "Three months' vacation with pay is the answer," he said.

As a music critic of merit, Virgil always preferred composing to writing. But in Clifton Fadiman's judgment, Virgil is a born writer.

His 424-page autobiography, published in 1967 with the title *Virgil Thomson* by Virgil Thomson, received laudatory praise from connoisseurs. A different reaction, however, came from Irving Kolodin, music editor of the *Saturday Review*. "Who wants to know that much about Virgil Thomson?" he asked.

When I was a prominent citizen, there was the customary cyclical craze—it still prevails—about asking people what they would take with them to a desert island. The reply of André Gide was books—old and new ones. The classic answer was that of Madeleine Carroll, the one-time movie star, who said she would take an obstetrician. As for me, since my nose was always running at the time because of my drug-taking, I said I would bring ten boxes of Kleenex.

The stories about W. Somerset Maugham have begun to come out. More will appear as the years go by. He was a writer who is now ignored by the critics in the United States and England, but he is still widely read and acclaimed over the rest of the world. I recall that Ada Leverson, the friend of Oscar Wilde, wrote six novels. I, in accordance with my custom, read five of them; one was a satire on Maugham.

I understand that after his death in 1965, Maugham's villa La Mauresque at Cap Ferrat on the French Riviera was put up for sale for about 420,000 pounds or nearly $1,800,000. It was originally built in 1906 by King Leopold II of Belgium for his chaplain. Maugham bought it twenty years later for a mere $50,000. It became, under his eye, a marvelous spot—very well-appointed, with a beautiful collection of paintings. But Maugham also wanted a fresh-water swimming pool, mostly for his visitors.

At the time, the village was under the domination of the French Communists. They, of course, refused to bow to the whim of such a famous capitalist. Thereupon Maugham and the mayor had a conference. Maugham emerged victorious. He had managed to bribe the mayor with the equivalent of $8000. "I don't mind corruption," Maugham said, shaking his head, "but really, on such a small scale!"

In his latter days Maugham became addicted to privacy. He made a fetish of ordering visitors and photographers off the place. He and Churchill were fond of each other, but Maugham dreaded the visits of the statesman and his retinue of newsmen and picture-takers. Once he literally hid in a closet. Though he was only ten months older than Churchill, he usually treated him like a spoiled younger brother, especially loathing his big prop cigars and V-fingers.

At the age of ninety-plus, Maugham's memory sometimes deserted him. But he never fretted about it; he knew it would return. His conversation became rather repetitive, punctuated with long silences. At this time George Cukor, the Hollywood director, visited him with the information that Warner Brothers had plans under way to make a picture out of his book *Cakes and Ale,* generally considered the second best of his works. Maugham pondered awhile, as if recalling the book, then said abruptly: "But there's no story in it."

At one time Maugham seriously considered making S. N. Behrman his literary executor and definitive biographer. Behrman told me he was afraid to do it because the old writer was so cantankerous. Maugham had added that, above all, he did not want his nephew Robin to write about him. Which of course is exactly what happened. The book was far from complimentary, though Robin wrote: "I have tried to be as kind as possible about my Uncle Willie."

Maugham told Behrman that "everything in life is an accident." He found out by experience what the philosophers had thought in theory. He also said that the usual method of homosexual writers was simply to substitute "she" for "he."

At a tea in the mid-fifties with Aldous Huxley, short-story genius John Collier, Christopher Isherwood, and Dame Edith Sitwell, I listened to the fascinating conversation and at last ventured to say that probably Noel Coward had succeeded Maugham as a successful playwright.

"Poor Willie!" shrieked Dame Edith in her inimitable voice.

At that time, Dame Edith had been hired by Columbia Pictures to write an original film. It was to be a secret project, the life of Anne Boleyn. She gave it her own title disguise: *The Life of Elizabeth the Great Until the Age of Two.*

The English seem to have unusual ideas about what constitutes the right to talent. I have always admired the Sitwells, right down the line of Osbert, Sacheverell, and Edith, but when I asked an English publisher about them, he answered contemptuously: "They were only knighted in the nineteenth century." I suppose that was about the time the peerage became generally known as the "beerage" because of the number of wealthy brewers who advanced in nobility.

When Sir Osbert came to the United States, he lectured across the country. After his encounter with San Francisco, he said: "I cannot overestimate the stupidity of the people." He used to deliberately speak very softly during his lectures and then raise his voice to inquire solicitously: "Can you hear me?"

"No!" the chorus would come back.

"Too bad," Osbert would say delightedly and continue.

As for Huxley himself, in his advanced years he was one of the most handsome and serene men I have ever seen. It was actress Iris Tree who told me that when Huxley was young he was one of the most stoop-shouldered, sunken-chested people *she* had ever seen. He had built up his physique and psychological equilibrium entirely by his own efforts.

Although he was virtually blind in his old age, Huxley always refused to admit it. He was usually accompanied by his wife or his son, yet he would not admit any physical handicap and his friends gave no help and no indication that they had seen it. Huxley would have hated them.

I asked Isherwood why Huxley had stopped writing novels in the full spate of his career. Isherwood said: "Because he wanted to spell out his philosophy and he did not want to be bothered by the dramatic trappings that are necessary for a novel."

A poignant line of Huxley's from his play *The Gioconda Smile,* "I'll never forgive Modigliani for dying so young," was picked up and used by—and about—others.

My own theory as to why Huxley took LSD is that it must have given him the vision his eyes no longer had. Huxley's death occurred at the time of the Kennedy assassination; consequently it was almost overlooked. His friend Isherwood disclosed that his last days were made serene by the use of the drug.

I was grateful to Isherwood for introducing me to his friend, the writer Stephen Spender. I invited him to appear on my TV show, and we discussed various authors. I recited from Shaw's

Doctor's Dilemma the creed uttered by one of his characters: "I believe in Michael Angelo, Velasquez, and Rembrandt."

"That was playing it safe," said Spender cynically.

In a published exchange between Spender and T. S. Eliot, the latter stated that it was impossible to be both a novelist and a poet. "Between us," he said to Spender, "Thomas Hardy was an amateur." (An opinion, incidentally, not shared by Isherwood.)

As someone said, when T. S. Eliot was young his poems were middle-aged, when he was middle-aged his poems were old, and when he was old his poetry was posthumous.

I heartily agree with Eliot's remark, "One must do something to soften the harshness of reality." The question, though, is what?

Christopher Isherwood was one of the British literary colony who shared the responsibility for taking care of Dylan Thomas when he came to Los Angeles for the first time in 1950. It was his first American poetry recital tour of universities and colleges.

Dylan checked into the Biltmore Hotel and put in a plaintive call to Christopher. "Which one of those big red buses do I have to take to get to UCLA?" he asked.

Christopher was shocked that no transportation had been provided for the eminent poet. "Wait right there," he said. "I'll come and get you." He also managed to fulfill Dylan's other request for "some booze and a blonde." The booze was easy enough to supply; the blonde was provided in person by Miss Shelley Winters, the actress. But Dylan found out to his chagrin that Shelley's interest in poetry did not extend to the poet.

Most visiting intellectuals to Hollywood in those days usually expressed interest in Charlie Chaplin and the Marx Brothers. Dylan was no exception. A longtime fan of Chaplin's, he was delighted to meet his hero.

When he gave his poetry reading at UCLA, Christopher said

Dylan was drunk right up to curtain time, yet once he walked on stage he became transformed. His artistry at reading poetry (his and other poetic works), coupled with his magnificent speaking voice, made for a tremendous evening. His drunken and lecherous behavior is too well known to recount, but off the lecture platform, according to writer Gore Vidal, "like all drunks, Dylan was a bore."

Of course that was his tragedy. His appalling self-destruction killed him at the age of thirty-nine. But his poems, in particular "Do Not Go Gentle into That Good Night," will surely endure.

When Christopher Isherwood was working at MGM Studios, I introduced him to Judy Garland. She paid him the most extravagant compliments. She told him how great he was, how wonderful his writings were, and what a genius he was. To which Christopher kindly replied, "Need I say the obvious in return?" It was the nearly perfect answer.

Isherwood told me that my *Memoirs* had passages which reminded him of *The Great Gatsby* by Scott Fitzgerald. I said somewhat plaintively, "Does that mean I have to fall in love with Sheilah Graham?"

At a large party a few years back we encountered a doctor from a Santa Monica hospital. Isherwood and I took an immediate dislike to him. It was after the death of J.F.K., and the doctor had the indecency to tell the guests that the assassination had not displeased him.

Christopher has for many years made his permanent home in Santa Monica. He confided to me that he expected to live a long time (his mother is in her nineties). But the idea that he might get sick and become a patient of this same doctor filled him with gloom. I tried to cheer him up; I said he would probably get sick somewhere else.

He took part in my adventures on television. I used to dictate its language in special, flowery, TV tones—full of multifarious sesquipedalian polysyllabics to indicate the degree of intelligence on my program. I often produced Christopher for conversation. He looked like a tweedy Will Rogers and sounded like a poetic Huckleberry Finn. Almost every time he appeared he used his favorite word "Alas!" with a sigh. It referred to our private joke. André Gide, in his memoirs, had said that the greatest poet in France was "Victor Hugo, alas!" Christopher would always say, "Alas, Baudelaire," and I would take great pleasure in correcting him. Christopher's sophisticated gee-whiz style was never more apparent than when I asked him for his opinion of *Lolita*. "Oh, gosh," he enthused, "what a marvelous guide to motels!"

Incidentally, at one period I delighted in the dark, lovely poetry of Baudelaire. His description of going insane appealed to my recurrent melancholia: "I cultivate my hysteria with terror and delight. Today I have received a singular warning—The wind of the wing of madness has passed over me."

Baudelaire never married but had an octoroon mistress with a wonderful name that sounds straight out of the Ziegfeld Follies: Jeanne Duval.

On my television show Isherwood also related a story involving the daughter of the great German author Thomas Mann. In Europe, Erika Mann had been a stranded refugee from Hitler's regime. "She had no nationality," recalled Isherwood. As an old friend of the family, he arranged for Erika to marry his friend, the English poet W. H. Auden. It was strictly a marriage of convenience to get Erika a passport.

Much later, when they all made their home in Southern California, Christopher was present when the Mann family was being photographed for a national magazine. Thomas Mann, as the patriarch, invited him to join the group. When the photographer inquired as to Christopher's identity, Mann announced with vast amusement, "Why, he is the family marriage broker!"

I never met any of the Mann family, but once, traveling on a cross-country train, I saw an extremely sensitive-faced girl reading in the lounge car. I said to myself, "That must be Erika Mann." I went across and asked her. It turned out to be her sister Elizabeth Borgese, which was still pretty close.

When the Los Angeles *Times* panned Isherwood's latest work as "decadent," Gore Vidal came to his defense. "Christopher is never decadent," said Gore loftily. "The reviewers for the L.A. *Times* are decadent." Gore, whom I recently described as the most exhilarating bastard around, does not dislike, he tolerates, reviewers.

In 1960, when Gore Vidal ran (and was defeated) for Congress from staid Republican Dutchess County in New York, he appeared with me on television. I asked him with devious ingenuousness, "Could Oscar Wilde have carried Dutchess County?" He fielded the query very well.

Once I declared to Gore that having affairs with a couple of women happened to bore me. "Are you a crypto homosexual?" he demanded evilly. I should say that his and Truman Capote's literary rivalry is as deep and immortal as any rivalry between the Greek gods. They both started as boy prodigies and ran neck and neck through the years. Gore had his triumph with *Julian;* Truman followed with his smash best seller *In Cold Blood.* Gore immediately left for Paris.

When he returned to California for a brief period, he announced, "I've just written two flop movies and a novel"; the novel turned out to be *Washington, D.C.* Even though it was faulted by the critics, Gore had the satisfaction of a big best seller. I asked him about a mutual friend, Paul Bowles, who is, I believe, one of the fine writers of our day. His books *The Sheltering Sky* and *The Delicate Prey* are already classics of their kind. Paul has made his home in Tangiers for many years and was formerly a hashish addict.

"Who is in worse shape," I demanded of Gore, "Bowles or myself?" He replied, "You are, Oscar."

It was a great comfort to me.

Chapter 8

$\mathcal{L}$YTTON Strachey, the English biographer and historian—he wrote *Eminent Victorians*—was one of the first real debunkers of history. He viewed the field of the past with a skeptical eye and wrote without favor. He had a tremendous public in the titillated twenties.

Strachey himself was called up for service in World War I. A member of the Bloomsbury Group, he was not exactly a masculine character, as was well known in the inner literary circles. This kind of personality was in itself a bar to becoming a member of the armed forces in those times. To make it worse, he had a high piping voice.

"What," demanded a basso profundo member of the draft

board, "would you do, sir, if a German soldier tried to rape your sister?"

"I would come between them," squeaked Strachey.

The story of Ronald Firbank is somewhat the same. I was one of his early fans. He was discovered originally when one of his books got a very bad review. The reviewer, fortunately for Firbank, quoted some of his lines. These attracted the attention of Osbert Sitwell, a discoverer of talent, and Firbank was on his way out of obscurity.

Firbank was also called up for service in World War I. He was rejected twice out of hand. The third time he was summoned, he indignantly sued the government for invasion of his privacy. Firbank was a precious writer in every sense of the word. He was converted to Catholicism in 1908; he died in Rome in 1926. He would not allow visitors into the room—not out of sentiment but because he said the wallpaper pattern was so dreadful.

It must have been hard to describe the mood of England in the First World War. The country went into it with such a feeling of romanticism. It emerged thoroughly sobered, a nation with a hangover that has lasted to this day. The prevailing mood of World War II was something out of the past. It carried through from 1914 to 1939, some twenty-five years before. No bravado, simply a grim resoluteness that did not dare to waver.

World War I was a very bad war for England. It was especially exemplified in the Gallipoli campaign that was invented by Winston Churchill. Many Englishmen had died in the trenches of France, but the cream of English youth was destroyed against Turkey along the Dardanelles. What's more, no real national hero ever came out of that conflict.

One English friend told me that if the Kaiser had won World War I, he would have appointed Lloyd George as the führer of his English province. I tend to doubt the truth of it. Not that I know too much about Lloyd George, but I did hear an interesting story from Chaim Weizmann. Weizmann, whose inventions (synthetic acetones for explosives) on the English side materially helped that country win World War I and was largely responsible for the nation of Israel today, told me that he had an appointment with Lloyd George. It fell on the day that the World War I armistice was declared. Weizmann said that the Prime Minister was true to his word and kept his appointment despite the instant mass celebrations. Weizmann was much moved by this fact.

I may make mistakes in my war estimates, but I hardly think they will be of the caliber made by the first Mrs. Douglas MacArthur. When she divorced the general to marry Lionel Atwill, the stage star, she said cheerily: "I'm trading in three little stars for one big one." I suppose she had her reasons, but no lady in history, as far as I know, has been so wretched a prophet —except the Queen of Sheba.

The twenties were the days when Americans were naïve enough to think that Communism was simply an idealistic doctrine. Perhaps the first joke Americans heard about it that had a real sting was the one concerning Feodor Chaliapin in Moscow. Chaliapin always starred in his favorite opera, *Boris Godunov*. Before one performance, the story ran, Chaliapin approached one of the Russian ushers.

"We are all equals now, eh?" he said.

"Yes, Comrade Chaliapin," returned the usher.

"Good!" thundered Chaliapin. "Tonight I shall be an usher. You play Boris!"

Like all wars, the campaigns of World War II will be endlessly argued about. For what they are worth, herewith are some opinions gathered from listening to hours of military gossip:

MONTGOMERY: In the Battle of the Bulge, General Bradley waited endlessly for the troops of Montgomery to appear. He should have known better. It was a congenital weakness of

Monty's that he never attacked—or even moved—until he had a vast, confirmed superiority over the enemy. He was hardly beloved by his staff officers. One of them declared openly that the only reason Montgomery won the African campaign was that the Nazi general Rommel had left before Montgomery began.

CLARK: A poor general with no imagination. His continued, head-on attacks on Monte Cassino in the Italian campaign lost thousands of crack American troops.

EISENHOWER: Perhaps a great general but certainly a great diplomat. He welded together very diverse groups of men. He never allowed any anti-American or any anti-English remarks. He always kept the whole staff on a perfectly even keel.

When France fell, everyone in the writing business wrote a book called *I Saw France Fall.* I want to say that possibly I should write a book entitled *I Saw Bix Beiderbeck Play the Horn,* but I did not see France fall.

I know an Englishman named Sir Solly Zuckerman. His name is not Solomon, just Solly. The title was attached to the Solly some time afterward. He is the keeper of the Royal Zoo in England and has various other important jobs.

I first knew Solly in 1933 when he gave a special course at Yale in anthropology. He also had gone through medical school, but never practiced medicine. He used to stay with the Gershwins and still does when he comes to the United States. They order special wines and cigars for him—which, by the way, they never do for me. (The fact that I don't drink and only smoke cigarettes may have something to do with it.) Solly always carried under his arm some novel by George Gissing, who used to write grim novels about the plight of the poor in Victorian England.

Once I asked Solly whatever had happened to John Strachey, a minor English literary figure. "Oh," Solly said blandly, "he became a member of Parliament and is now entirely forgotten."

During World War II Solly was assigned to Lord Louis Mountbatten's staff in an advisory capacity. Mountbatten was reported to have been slightly bewildered to learn that his new staff member was the author of a book entitled *Functional Affinities of Man, Monkeys and Apes*.

Sir Solly also served as an advisor to General Eisenhower. In a little island off the coast of Italy, he was the first person to work on pinpoint bombing.

I asked Solly who had planned the operations for D-Day. "Some brigadier general named Morgan," he told me. Later this same officer was put in charge of part of occupied Germany and was subsequently removed for anti-Semitism.

The day that Hitler invaded Russia—why is it that no one ever says Hitler invaded Stalin or Germany invaded Stalin?—as I recollect it, I was sitting with a group in Lindy's restaurant in New York. Harry Hopkins came in and sat with us. He was a great man, one of my first heroes; it was hard for me to see how anyone in the world could think otherwise of him. He looked thin and tired.

"General Marshall gives Russia six weeks," he said.

He looked at me. "We need those six weeks," he added grimly. It was true. We needed every second we could get that would enable us to prepare for the inevitable.

Eric Ambler, who served in World War II as a colonel, was attached for a time to Churchill and his staff at Chequers, the weekend retreat of prime ministers. One of Ambler's duties was to report to his boss the name of the Sunday night movie.

In those days, for some unfathomable reason, Churchill was very high on the saccharine Deanna Durbin pictures which Joe Pasternak produced in the *Wienerschmalz* tradition. Churchill's favorite was *A Hundred Men and a Girl;* throughout the picture he had muttered appreciatively, "Very talented girl—very talented girl."

He was happily anticipating another Durbin picture for the

following week. Ambler came in and saluted smartly. "Sir," he said, "the picture next week will be *Bachelor Mother,* with Ginger Rogers."

Churchill was stunned. He leveled his finger at Ambler and said with his thunderous stutter: "I have been notified otherwise. We shall see, we shall see!" There is no record of whether or not he got his wish. But it reminds me that General Sherman's immortal remark, "War is hell," caused Churchill to say, "He made it so!"

Vic Oliver, the music hall entertainer and onetime husband of Sarah Churchill, was not her father's favorite. On a walk together at Chequers, Oliver asked the Prime Minister whom he admired in the war. Without hesitation, Churchill growled "Mussolini! He had the courage to have his son-in-law shot." He was referring, of course, to Count Ciano, the foreign minister of Italy before he fell out of favor with Il Duce.

Lady Astor, the witty and acerbic member of Parliament, once said to Churchill in exasperation: "If I were married to you, I would put cyanide in your tea!"

To which Churchill replied, "If I were married to you, I would drink it!"

A dramatic incident of the war days took place at Brentano's bookstore in Washington. One of the customers had fallen and injured herself. She claimed to be Mrs. Winston Churchill and asked that the White House be notified. Of course, no one believed her—a visit by the Prime Minister and his lady would have been common knowledge.

It was Frank McCarthy, assistant to General Marshall, who happened by and recognized that the lady was indeed Mrs. Churchill. The Churchills' trip had been one of utmost secrecy.

There is, of course, the never-sufficiently circulated story about another Churchill visit to the White House. F.D.R., so it goes, wheeled himself up to Churchill's bedroom and opened the door unexpectedly. He was startled to find the Prime Minister in the middle of the room, entirely naked except for a cigar.

Churchill was not in the least discomposed. He spread his hands and rumbled with disingenuous frankness: "You see, Mr. President, we British have nothing to hide."

Churchill was in his eighties and still an M.P. when he decided to visit the House of Parliament. The appearance of the former Prime Minister created a stir, diverting attention from the discussion of a public housing bill then in progress.

A few of the members became annoyed at the interruption. Clucked one of them irritably, "After all, they say he is potty!"

"They say he can't hear either!" came the thunderous Churchill rumble.

It may not be too well known about Churchill's written request that "The Battle Hymn of the Republic" be sung at his funeral services. When it began, the English were not too pleased to hear an American Civil War song. But as the number progressed, the sweep of the music and heroic phrases stirred the listeners deeply. It was a fitting tribute to Churchill's American ancestry.

Former President Eisenhower revealed on a 1967 television program that the two greatest men he ever knew were Churchill and General George Catlett Marshall. His other accolade went to General Bradley as the best field general in World War II.

I asked Averell Harriman who in his opinion was the greater, F.D.R. or Churchill. He said with complete certitude, "Roosevelt with the help of General Marshall made every important decision." Justice William O. Douglas told me the same thing—which I invariably repeat to my English friends to see them turn livid with disagreement. Harriman told me that F.D.R., during his terms, was the leader not only of the United States; he thought in terms of the whole world. In all fairness to Churchill, however, he was seldom in a position to override Roosevelt. With his impossible dream, Churchill was the Don Quixote of world leaders.

Averell Harriman is one of the men I most admire. He is a selfless, distinguished public servant of the best kind. But his judgment on his own future is sometimes at fault: two weeks before the 1960 Rockefeller landslide election, he was still convinced that he would be reelected governor of New York.

His judgment on foreign affairs, however, is impeccable. It is always Harriman who flies around the world performing confidential business for the current President. One of his disadvantages is that he is so self-effacing that he retires after each administration. He has to wait for his virtues to be recognized all over again. And he does not even have a law practice to fall back on, as most politicians do, although of course he is a very rich man.

In the old days I was always invited, with hordes of their friends, to the Harrimans' traditional Thanksgiving Day celebration. It was held at their place in upstate New York. As fond of them as I am, country life didn't interest me, but I did go once with Beatrice Kaufman. Heywood Broun, the celebrated newspaper columnist who had been instrumental, with Morris Ernst, in forming the New York Newspaper Guild, spent most of his time in the kitchen trying to unionize the help. Charlie Lederer, the cutup and caper kid, had fun after everyone went to bed, switching around the shoes that were left outside the doors.

I couldn't stand the gamy food that was served; I suppose it was venison or some such thing, but at midnight the scrambled eggs cooked personally by Averell were delicious.

Marie Harriman, a warm and outspoken woman, had an art gallery in the city, as a hobby and an expression of her taste. Unfortunately, her poor eyesight prevented her from accompanying her husband on two important posts—his ambassadorship to Russia as well as England. Harriman's daughter Kathleen served as his hostess instead.

I once had a secret meeting with Harriman as he discussed the possibility of my writing a weekly piece for *Newsweek*. I was too involved in concert work to accept, but I was flattered by the offer. Harriman must have been connected with the magazine in some unknown proprietary way. Anyway, John O'Hara was given the assignment. I remember he wrote a piece blasting the New York drama critic Brooks Atkinson, who had blasted O'Hara's show *Pal Joey*. That show had created a new mold in musical shows with the leading man a new type of heel-hero. Revivals prove its viability.

In the *Newsweek* article, O'Hara angrily wrote that he was going to punch Brooks Atkinson in the nose. He must have been dissuaded, Atkinson then being about four feet tall and weighing two pounds.

Among Harriman's private victories I may mention two. He and his partner always beat Eisenhower and his favorite partner, General Gruening, the head of NATO, at bridge. And it was he and his wife who reared Peter Duchin, the son of Eddy Duchin, after the latter's tragic death. Harriman's warmheartedness makes him beloved by all his friends.

When President Truman appointed Averell Harriman as Secretary of Commerce, Harriman, on the advice of Herbert Bayard Swope, made George Backer his adviser. George remained in this capacity throughout Harriman's term as Governor of New York. Backer then became a leader of the reform movement in New York City's Democratic party.

George Backer and I, introduced by our mutual friend Sam Behrman, have been friends since the twenties. A member of a wealthy family, George was (and is) handsome and equable of temperament, with an interest in politics and sociology. Behrman and I would kid him about his hero worship of Disraeli— a framed letter of his idol hung over his bed.

When Behrman was in California around 1931, toiling for MGM, George and I went out to visit him. Behrman worked at the studio most of the time, so George and I would play a little handball and wait for the four-day-old New York *Times* to arrive. We found it all pretty boring.

Backer was also adored by Alexander Woollcott, not only for his intelligence but for his comforting, calm, and reflective personality.

On his return to New York from a Florida visit, George announced that he had met an "Egyptian princess." (This was long before the Israeli problem!) He had met Dorothy Schiff, the exotic and handsome daughter of the affluent Mortimer Schiff, and they were married soon after. Woollcott was upset by the marriage—his proprietory claim on his friends could be that intense.

It was George Backer's idea that his wife should buy the New York *Post* which, incidentally, in those days was not a tabloid. The first person that Backer hired when he became the publisher of the paper was Heywood Broun, a writer for the *World Telegram*. On that paper his column had appeared above the column of Westbrook Pegler, who publicly vilified Broun for organizing the Newspaper Guild. But Pegler vilified everybody. When Broun's column was placed below Pegler's, the ignominy was complete; Broun switched to the *Post*. Two days later he tragically died of pneumonia.

Franklin P. Adams worked most of his career for the *Herald Tribune* and then asked for a raise. The editors refused him. So he fled to the columns of the New York *Post*. He admitted to me afterward that the change had not done him any good except in a cash way. Most of his column was a strip of paste-ups out of the mail anyway, and he said disconsolately: "Practically all my mail comes from Washington Heights." He got more money, but he had to work a lot harder; he had gotten much higher-class mail with much better contributions when he was with the *Tribune*. Like reviews, it is not only the critic or the columnist, it is the paper that prints the stuff which makes the difference.

George Backer was best man at my first wedding. After the ceremony we went to the Ritz Carlton Hotel for coffee and brioche. After my divorce, as a matter of sentiment, I never ate brioche again. (Which reminds me of Marie Antoinette's remark. She didn't say, "Let them eat cake"; she said, "Let them eat brioche.")

Backer's marriage did not survive either. At one point in their lives, Dolly Backer (as she was known then) announced angrily that she was going to Europe. Ever-imperturbable George casually replied, "Pick up some shirts for me in London."

The day his divorce was final, George went straight to the induction center to enlist. He took the customary medical exam and was told, to his horror, that he had tuberculosis. That, I would say, was a fairly dramatic day in one man's life!

Anyway, it all turned out all right. George eventually recovered and went overseas to join the Office of War Information (probably singing "Good-bye, Dolly").

After the Backer-Schiff marriage dissolved, Dolly Schiff continued as the publisher of the New York *Post*. Little more than a dilettante when she started, she developed enormous ability and courage, successfully steering the paper through every crisis. The *Post* is as of now the only afternoon paper left in New York.

In 1952 I was on a train (that dying method of transportation) going to the West Coast. Everybody else on the train was going to the political convention in Chicago, including Dorothy Schiff. We had dinner together. She wrote later in her column that she was dying to interview Herbert Hoover at the other end of the car—but that she had to be content with Oscar Levant.

The stopover in Chicago gave me the pleasure of renewing my acquaintance with Mr. and Mrs. Eugene Meyer and their daughter and son-in-law, Kay and Philip Graham. They had come from Washington to attend the convention.

Eugene Meyer, a onetime member of the Hoover administration, had acquired in the thirties the foundering Washington *Post*. For years it lost five million dollars annually; in time it became one of the finest papers in the country.

I had met the Meyers for the first time when Sam Behrman (again) and I spent a weekend at their home at Mt. Kisco, New York. Young and bumptious, I amused the multi-millionaire with my first remark: "I'd like to trade trust funds with you." My weekend outfit, blue corduroy trousers, fake-gem-studded belt, an African pith helmet on my head, provoked a Belgian banker guest to venture the opinion that I looked like an adventurer. My idiosyncrasies did not deceive Mrs. Meyer, however.

She proved astute when she decribed me as "insular." Whatever the appellation, I must have been a bizarre figure unfettered by the lack of success.

When Eugene Meyer died, Phil Graham, a bright, personable young man, took over the reins of the Washington *Post*. The Meyer family also acquired *Newsweek*, developing the magazine into a rival of *Time*. (It is often superior.)

The tragic illness and ultimate suicide of Phil Graham, during the Kennedy administration, shocked not only the Washington inner circle but the journalistic world as well. Kay Graham, a vital part of the organization, then became the head of the Meyer enterprises.

Mrs. Agnes Meyer, the matriarch of the family, has always been a dominating, formidable woman involved in many activities. When Walter Lippmann wrote an article disapproving the nomination of John F. Kennedy, Mrs. Meyer retaliated by revealing in print that Lippmann had supported Landon back in 1936. In any event, the elder statesman of political journalists was signed, shortly after that, to write for the Washington *Post* syndicate.

In his youth, when Lippmann was a writer for the weekly magazine *New Republic,* he was tapped by Herbert Bayard Swope for the New York *World.* Accustomed to a weekly piece, Lippmann at first declined the offer, concerned by the demands of a daily newspaper deadline. He eventually capitulated and joined the paper as a member of the editorial staff.

I saw a good deal of Herbert Swope in the war days. He was the first newspaperman to get the Pulitzer Prize. He was not responsible for the folding of the old New York *World;* he left it a year before it went under. He always claimed that he told Joseph Pulitzer that it would still sell if he raised the price to a dime per copy.

Swope used to ghostwrite all of Al Smith's speeches (as far as I know, Woodrow Wilson was the last politician who wrote his own speeches, and that is a long while back). One night he and a friend were listening to Smith speak. When it was over, his unknowing friend turned and said to Swope: "What a terrible speech that was!" It was one of Swope's two most awkward moments—when he could neither agree nor disagree. The other moment came when he lost a bet on the pronunciation of "impious." It is pronounced *im*pious, and Swope always claimed it was the only bet he ever lost.

His moments of real satisfaction came at the dinner table, surrounded by what seemed to be hundreds of guests, cronies, dignitaries, or freeloaders. At least once during every meal Swope would boom unctuously: "Gentlemen, it is lawful to rape your wife." Nearly as famous as that line was his misty description of something he happened to like: "Gentlemen, it was touched with beauty."

It was about one of Swope's rich Jewish friends that I observed, "He can afford every luxury except anti-Semitism."

At another Swope evening, the man who owned the *New Yorker* magazine, Raoul Fleischman, insisted on telling me about his ex-wife.

"She didn't like you," he volunteered.

"She didn't like you, either," I reminded him.

In 1954, when I was in deep brouhaha with the Musicians Union, Leonard Lyons invested the aid of Senator Hubert Humphrey, who said he would help me. He never did. Then Leonard tried George Meany, head of the AFL-CIO. He gave the same reassurances. I told James Petrillo, head of the American Federation of Musicians, that Meany was coming to my aid. Petrillo snorted and said: "Meany, hell! We hire him!"

Swope wrote me a letter commiserating with me on my troubles. He summed up his feelings thusly: "It seems to me, from the public standpoint, you'd be justified in throwing out Petrillo instead of having that process reversed." And he signed his name with the customary red pencil: Onkle Herbert.

George Sokolsky, the right-wing columnist, wrote the best obituary of Swope when he died. Sokolsky got very mellow just before his own death. He forgot or forgave all his feuds; he even liked President Kennedy. It was Sokolsky who converted more Communists to capitalism than Billy Graham did atheists to religion.

A wonderful story was told to me by Paul Porter, a Washington lawyer and political insider. It was about the Truman-Dewey election campaign of 1948. (That was the year I got one bad review in Washington because I was accused of "impudent raillery" with some kids in the box at one of my concerts.) The Porter story concerned the days when Dewey was staying in New York at the Waldorf-Astoria. Frank Sinatra, who was then at the height of his squealing popularity, was staying there as well. He was a rabid Democratic supporter.

Porter and his helpers made arrangements to have Sinatra on hand whenever Dewey came downstairs. Dewey descended; the signal was given. Lo! Sinatra appeared—at the door farthest away from the one where Dewey would enter. Everyone in the lobby would shriek and rush to see Sinatra come in. It left Dewey looking alone and chagrined.

In the long-gone days when Robert M. Hutchins taught rather than pontificated, he was, at the age of twenty-eight, the dean of the Yale Law School. One of his pupils was Herbert Brownell, later the sponsor of Thomas Dewey for President and Attorney General under Eisenhower. Asked about this, Hutchins replied solemnly: "I must have been a very poor teacher." On the other or anti-Hutchins side, I recall someone saying: "Hutchins considers a discussion on the fate of one nation merely small talk."

As a dropout myself, I have never been impressed with the educational qualifications necessary for outstanding democratic leaders and good common sense. I realize that Thomas Jefferson founded the University of Virginia and that Wilson was a professor and president of Princeton, but they were exceptions. It is generally known that J.F.K. made very bad marks his first three years at Harvard. It is not as well known that F.D.R. flunked his bar examinations three times in a row. Dwight D. Eisenhower's average marks at West Point were ordinary. Harry Truman wasn't noted for his scholastic triumphs.

If this country had to depend on college diplomas in high places, we might be pretty badly off.

As far as F.D.R. was concerned, he certainly owed much of his extraordinary confidence to his mother. As her only child, she taught him to express himself freely. Whatever he had to say, she made him feel it was worthwhile. A valuable legacy.

I remember meeting Mrs. Sara Delano Roosevelt at a special screening of the Orson Welles movie *Citizen Kane*, a thinly disguised story of the journalistic colossus, William Randolph

Hearst. When asked for her opinion, Mrs. Roosevelt was definite. "It should not have been made in his lifetime," she said.

On the day of his 1933 inauguration, F.D.R. respectfully paid a visit to the retired and elderly (in his nineties) Justice Oliver Wendell Holmes. After the President departed, Holmes turned to his aide and asked in bewilderment, "Who was that young man?"

J.F.K. said that no previous experience ever prepared anyone for the Presidency. I have to disagree. F.D.R. was ready for the job on the very day he took office. In 1940 I voted for my first time. I was quite fervent about F.D.R. The press appeared at the polling place, and they insisted, for publicity's sake (I was on the radio program *Information Please*), that I be given a literacy test.

I had first seen President Roosevelt at a Madison Square Garden rally and had realized anew the enormous physical handicap with which he was burdened. He held onto the lectern and used his head to punctuate his points—a characteristic mannerism even when he was seated.

I saw him again at a Waldorf-Astoria Hotel banquet the night of the day he rode, old and sick, in an open car in the rain.

January, 1945, because of a heavy concert schedule, I was unable to attend the inauguration ceremonies for President Roosevelt. Nor could I accept an invitation to meet Mrs. Roosevelt at the White House. Yet I probably admired both of them more than any two people in my lifetime.

May, 1945, at a whistle-stop town in Texas, a newsboy on the train platform held up a special edition of a newspaper proclaiming the death of President Roosevelt.

It has been said that there is a decade in a man's life that shapes him forever. My decade was the Roosevelt years.

As F.D.R. was my first and great political idol, his father figure image will always be firmly etched in my mind. But the other object of my political admiration was Adlai Stevenson. His brilliant 1952 acceptance speech after his first nomination was a revelation.

My wife and I met the Governor of Illinois for the first time in February, 1956, at the Los Angeles home of the Edward Laskers. The occasion was a private dinner party in honor of the distinguished visitor's birthday. (His birthplace, incidentally, was Los Angeles.)

June, also a great admirer of Stevenson's, had just read the book *My Brother Adlai*, written by his sister, Mrs. Elizabeth Ives. June did an unusual thing for her; she brought the book along to the party for an inscription—not that she would intrude on his privacy, she said, but should the right moment arise. . . .

We arrived at the Laskers, June left her book in the ladies' room, and we joined the gathering—a gala affair attended by many of the movieland great. After we were introduced to the Governor, June casually mentioned that she had read his sister's book. "Oh?" said the Governor with interest, "I haven't had time to read it. Is it any good?" She assured him that it was and told him that she had brought her book along in the hope that he would inscribe it for her. "How enchanting of you," he exclaimed, taking her arm. "Let's go get it."

She had to restrain him from marching to the ladies' room and promised she'd get the book later.

At his table, Stevenson was surrounded by beautiful movie actresses—his good friend Betty Bogart, Joan Fontaine, Ginger Rogers, Joan Caulfield, and of course the hostess, Jane Greer Lasker. I also noticed that my wife had several dances with him. What's more, she brought home her book inscribed: To June Levant with my heart!

In spite of his gaiety, this was Stevenson's second campaign for the Presidency, and his disillusionment was deep. A wizard with words, his own brilliant style was, by this time, considered too sophisticated by his advisors. In an attempt to be "down to earth" he mouthed the speeches written for him by others, bitter about the concessions he had to make. He went through the necessary motions, yet he knew that his defeat was inevitable. One of his writers was Arthur Schlesinger, Jr., who was to become a member of the John F. Kennedy political family four years later.

I next saw Stevenson at an MGM luncheon in the executive dining room, Dore Schary presiding. We exchanged a few quips and had our picture taken together, and he sent a little note to June: "I'm still in love—are you? And can I entrust this to your husband?"

On my weekly Los Angeles television show of the time, I was a passionate vocal advocate of Stevenson. My pro-Stevenson and anti-Nixon remarks aroused resentment as well as glee. I noted that Stevenson talked over some people's heads, but then President Eisenhower sometimes talked over his own head.

In April, 1956, Stevenson was deep in the rigors of his campaign when he again stopped briefly in Los Angeles. I received the following handwritten note:

> Thank you, my dear friend, for that telephone call the other night in L.A.—which I wanted to return and couldn't in that rocketing chaos and with that appalling schedule—until 12 P.M., and then I decided to be merciful. But it was a difficult decision, because I *need* help in California and I believe you might have had helpful hints for an innocent and awkward politician!
>
> Thank you, sir. On to Florida!
>
> A.E.S.

The dramatic Democratic convention of 1960 will be long remembered. Averell Harriman was in Los Angeles as the leader of a Washington contingent determined to nominate Senator Kennedy. He appeared as a guest on my syndicated television show, predicting with absolute certainty that John F. Kennedy would be the Democratic nominee. At Averell's invitation, my wife and I attended a dinner at Chasen's restaurant that included members of the Washington entourage. (Among them, Mrs. Frances Lanihan, Scott Fitzgerald's daughter.) My wife was asked by a young Washington lawyer what she thought of the Senator's chances. June, a Stevenson supporter, gave him her frank opinion. "How can you expect a candidate, so little known by the majority of the American people, to beat Vice-president Nixon?" she asked.

The lawyer replied, "If Senator Kennedy were here right now, you would be bowled over by his eloquence."

She didn't believe him.

It was not until we witnessed the Nixon-Kennedy debates on television that she remembered the lawyer's prediction.

Bowled over was right!

After Kennedy became President, James Reston, my favorite political writer, related a conversation that he had with Averell Harriman. Harriman told Reston that he wished that President Kennedy would stop calling him Governor and start calling him Averell. But that seemed to be his fate, said Harriman; he had to start from scratch with each new President. However, Harriman added, he decided he'd follow Sam Goldwyn's advice: "Don't let it bother you. Don't even ignore it."

Arthur Krock, the dean of political writers, had known Jack Kennedy for many years. The young Kennedy had always been most respectful to the distinguished journalist, addressing him as Mr. Krock. When Kennedy assumed the Presidency, their positions were considerably altered. Furthermore, Krock wrote several pieces attacking Kennedy's policies. I was told that after one particular White House dinner, President Kennedy placed his arm affectionately around Krock's shoulder and said in his most ingratiating manner, "Tell me, Arthur, why do you write such bullshit?"

President Kennedy used his diplomacy in various ways. When Mrs. Kennedy redecorated the White House, she banished from sight a portrait of Mrs. Eisenhower that she considered an artistic blight. Some time later she was urgently summoned by the President.

"Quick," he said, "get that picture of Mamie back on the wall."

"Why, Jack?" she asked in surprise.

"They're coming for lunch," he explained.

After Mrs. Kennedy made such a smash hit on their European trip, the President took to calling her "the sex symbol." ("Is the S.S. ready?" he would teasingly inquire.)

Another time, when the Kennedys attended a horse show (incidentally, they bored the President to distraction), Gore Vidal was a member of their party. He was seated directly behind the President, who turned around and lightly remarked: "If anyone wanted to take a shot at me this would be a good place to do it."

"Yes," agreed Gore, "but they might get me instead!"

"That wouldn't be much of a loss," quipped Kennedy.

Gore Vidal, a remote relative of Mrs. Kennedy (something about his half-sister Nina sharing the same step-father as Jackie), fell out of favor with the family. I understand that it was precipitated when Gore put his arm around Jackie at some dinner or other. Bobby commanded, "Take your hands off the First Lady!" Whatever the reason for the rift, they are now deadly enemies, at least on Gore's side. And he never fails to denounce Bobby, publicly or otherwise.

The syndicated writer for the Los Angeles *Times,* Art Seidenbaum, once asked me how I could like Joe Kennedy. I said, "How can I resist liking a man who liked me so much?" I recounted to him that in 1958, after my long illness, I appeared on an Eddie Fisher television show. The first telegram I received had come from Hyannisport:

IT'S GREAT TO HAVE YOU BACK WHERE ALL OF US CAN SEE YOU. YOU

ARE STILL TOPS IN MY BOOK. DINNER WAITING FOR YOU AT PAVILLON
AT ANY TIME. BEST =

JOE KENNEDY

Although his near-fatal illness has left Joe Kennedy partially
disabled, I last saw him a couple of years ago at the Caravelle
restaurant in New York. We exchanged greetings, and as Senator Robert Kennedy shook my hand, he remarked, "I know
you are an old friend of my father's."

After their dinner, it was a touching sight to see Bobby
maneuvering his father's wheelchair out of the restaurant.

Incidentally, it was again Averell Harriman who was an important adviser to Robert Kennedy in his successful campaign
for Senator from New York. I sincerely hope that Bobby calls
him "Ave."

Bobby has been criticized for being too ambitious. He is
viewed with suspicion because he has his eye on the Presidency.
Well, what's the matter with that? It's the highest office in the
land. You'd think he wanted to join the Mafia!

To Bobby's defense came Harry Golden.

"If you want to judge a man, take a look at his enemies," he
said.

President Lyndon B. Johnson is not one of my favorite Presi-
dents. Carl Sandburg said it all when he commented: "This
Johnson, he's no McKinley." I join in his wife's beautification
program for the country; I also feel that it would be forwarded
if the Presidential family were kept out of sight. I was told that
when Bobby Kennedy was running for Senator, Johnson prayed
heartily for his defeat. The way things are going, Johnson may
have to start praying that Bobby won't be his Vice-president
in 1968.

Did you hear that Johnson said to Humphrey, "When I
want your advice I'll give it to you"?

In my opinion, the war in Vietnam was the fault of J.F.K.

and General Maxwell Taylor, who wrote the book *An Uncertain Trumpet.* He has always advocated small brush-wars as fashionable military procedure. He did so as chief of the Army under President Eisenhower and was eased out. Afterward, however, J.F.K. called him in and adopted his theories that led directly to Vietnam. To me there is no such thing as a "little" brush-war—just as there is no such thing as a woman being a little pregnant or a salad having a little garlic.

Seventy-five-year-old Senator George Aiken of Vermont said in the summer of 1967, "We should withdraw from Vietnam and two weeks later declare our victory. People have short memories."

I would certainly be in favor of that.

Chapter 9

IN the summer of 1967 Paul Gardner of the New York *Times* asked me to write a piece on television for a Sunday edition. As I was busy on this book, I had to decline, so Pamela Mason wrote a piece instead.

Her article, under the title "The Gift of Gab and How to Use It," dealt with TV talkers and was enhanced by Hirschfeld caricatures of her subjects: Johnny Carson, Zsa Zsa and Eva Gabor, Pamela, and I. She wrote:

A pastmaster at the art of giving an audience a peep at real life is Oscar Levant. Interviewing him and being interviewed by him are two of the most absorbing and hair-raising experiences that anyone in his right mind can have—and afterward he may not be in his right mind. Nobody can compare with Levant. You never know what he'll say or do next but you can be sure he will say or do *anything*—but amid these terrifying moments come the wittiest, most pointed remarks ever made by anybody on the air.

Pamela, an overwhelming unorthodox, eccentric Englishwoman, was a frequent guest on my TV shows of the fifties. I was pretty wild in those days, and she never forgot the experience.

I am my own worst critic. I remember once—and only once— I sat and writhed as I watched myself on a taped TV show. The only way I can describe it is that I was *meshuggah*—that is, nuts.

I recall the last time I was in New York, the fall of 1965. I did three shows in a row for Merv Griffin.

"Well, Oscar," said Merv on the first show, "how do you like being back in New York?"

"New York has everything, but you can't get in," I replied.

The discussion proceeded and finally Merv asked, "What would you do if you had your life to live over again?"

"I'd talk my parents out of it," I decided.

On another show, Steve Lawrence was a guest. I was delighted to meet him, as he and his wife Eydie Gorme are about my favorite singers. I also remembered a remark made about him by the actor Tom Poston. "Steve Lawrence," he said, "looks like Diana Dors, the English actress." He does, too.

Anyway, on this particular show Steve sang at my request, and beautifully, the Rodgers and Hart song "Where or When." He then joined in the conversation, recounting as performers usually do on talk shows some of the accidents that happen during the long run of a play.

In one anecdote, Steve dramatically built up the suspense about an unnamed actor who forgot his lines:

"His mind went blank," he recalled. "He turned *white—*"

"You must mean Sammy Davis, Jr.," I interjected helpfully.

June, my wife, appeared with me on these TV shows; my *Memoirs* had just been published, and we were supposed to mention the book—something I kept overlooking.

On one of the shows, June launched into a long stream of stories, talking her head off with all the aplomb in the world. As she paused for breath, I muttered to Merv, "I'm beginning to feel like Gordon MacRae."

When June came to a halt she whispered something to Merv.

"What did she say?" I asked curiously.

"She wants a glass of water," replied Merv, pouring it.

"*Water?* That's a strange request, coming from my wife!" I announced.

But it was all in fun.

I finally remembered why I was there. "Why not plug my book?" I said to Merv.

"It's a very good book," he said placatingly.

Then suddenly I was embarrassed.

"How do you know?" I cried. "Since when are you a literary critic?"

And so it went. Old Lovable.

June and I also appeared that year on the *Les Crane Show* when it was on the network. On that show, I remarked offhand that every modern composer in this country except one is a homosexual.

I was told later that if I had not used the word "one," the line would have been blooped. Without the saving word, it would have been considered a wholesale indictment.

Everyone wanted to know who the one was who was not; actually, there is more than one.

When I go to New York, I usually stay at the Algonquin Hotel, an unpretentious small hostelry on West Forty-fourth Street. It is a hotel with a tradition.

In the twenties, the Algonquin's fame as a literary hangout started when Alexander Woollcott, Franklin P. Adams, and

Heywood Broun began meeting there for a weekly lunch date. From that beginning the hotel blossomed into the favorite daily luncheon place of the wits, celebrities, and intellectuals of the period. I was not a member of the famous "round table," though I was later to become friends with many of its members.

Today the Algonquin, with its faded literary past, is far from "plushy," yet it still attracts renowned members of the theatrical world. Most of the stellar British actors and authors, from Hayley Mills to Sir Ralph Richardson, find its lack of chichi and its convenient location attractive.

When the English company of the movie *Dr. Zhivago* came to New York for the premiere performance, Geraldine Chaplin and others connected with the film were comfortably ensconced at the Waldorf-Astoria Towers. Not, however, Julie Christie. Against the wishes of the press department, I was amused to learn, she headed straight for the Algonquin.

Still, there are certain disadvantages connected with living there. Although the food is excellent, comparable to the finest New York hotel, on Sunday there is no hot food served after two P.M. Another thing, the hotel has only one passenger elevator.

After my wife and I had checked in on one visit, we were delayed in reaching our room by an interminable wait for the lone elevator. June complained to the bellhop.

"Charles Laughton stayed here for twenty-eight years," he informed her. "Nineteen of 'em were spent waiting for the elevator."

When we finally reached our rooms, I made my usual request to the maid for more blankets. "You see," I explained to her, "I didn't get much affection when I was a child."

The place may look a bit on the antiquated side, but the food prices are far from inexpensive. In any case, I never bothered checking over the bills; I just signed them. Our breakfasts on that trip were somewhat puzzling. My wife and I had exactly the same breakfast in our rooms each day. Each time, somehow, the bill was different.

At a dinner in New York I entertained some friends, and when the check came I did some rapid calculation. Putting several large-denomination bills atop the check, I asked my friend Leonard Lyons: "Do you think that a three hundred percent tip is enough from someone with an inferiority complex?"

After a show we went to a delicatessen for a sandwich and noticed the eminent customers arriving. They were actors, musicians, songwriters, directors, etc. "This place has become like a true international café," I explained to my wife, "except that they're all of one nationality."

One of my experiences with an amateur TV critic came when I was walking into the men's room at Toots Shor's restaurant. The man coming out stopped me.

"You're Oscar Levant," he said, as if making a discovery. I admitted it.

"You're on TV," he said.

"Thank you," I muttered automatically.

"That doesn't mean I *like* you!" he replied.

New York is not all wild fun, however. A few years ago June came back to the hotel from a tiring day of struggling through crowds, dirty streets, rain, and lack of cabs.

I was stretched out on the bed comfortably enjoying President Kennedy's press conference on television. As June sat down to listen, her earring fell off and rolled under the bed.

She got down on the floor to look for it, coming up in a second with a horrified squeal.

"There's a cigar under the bed!" she cried. That's right, there was a discarded, half-smoked cigar butt under the bed.

As we don't smoke cigars, and none of our visitors had, we could only assume that it had been left there by the former occupants.

"That does it!" said June, picking up the phone, "we're going *home!"*

She called our teen-aged daughters in California, told them the cigar incident, and informed them we'd be home that night.

"So soon?" they wailed. Naturally, they liked having the house to themselves for a change.

Afterward, we learned that one of our daughters suggested: "Let's put a cigar butt under mother's bed; maybe they'll go back to New York!"

You can't win.

It was around then that I appeared once in a while on a TV panel show called *Celebrity Game.* The format consisted of an assorted group of well-known people who were asked inane questions about love, sex and marriage. We got the questions in advance, and everyone except me, I finally discovered, was also provided with the answers. The writers obviously couldn't depend on the celebrities to be all that amusing on their own.

Carl Reiner acted as the moderator. That was the show when he made the decision to appear for the first time on TV without his toupee. But there was such a negative reaction to his bald pate from the viewers that after a few weeks of appearing *au naturel* he went back to his rug. A minor TV incident.

The technical expert for the questions submitted was Dr. Joyce Brothers, the lady psychiatrist who has become a familiar figure to television watchers and whom incidentally I have never met.

At the conclusion of one show, Carl Reiner was reeling off the names of the people responsible for the show. At the mention of Dr. Brothers' name I spoke up.

"She's been treating me for thirty years," I intoned.

There was a split-second pause as Carl Reiner digested this bit of unexpected and untrue information.

Then he rose to the occasion.

"And she's done a *good* job," he announced heartily, as the show went off the air.

It was also the show where Allan Sherman launched into such a spate of self-revelation that I asked in surprise: "Is this a documentary?"

The show was taped, so they cut that out.

On another show I met the international model Suzy Parker, and she and I and our spouses have been good friends ever since. Once at a dinner party, Suzy was seated between the indefatigable Groucho Marx and me—which means that no sentences were ever finished.

Johnny Carson dropped me a nice note after my *Memoirs* were published, in which he said that he had only read the last page of my book and yet with his unfailing instinct he knew it would be a best seller.

Although pleased, I was slightly puzzled by his assessment. Then I recalled that I had written one short anecdote about him in the book. It happened to appear on the last page.

I watched Artie Shaw, who has a record of seven marriages, on one of the *Tonight* shows. He was telling Johnny Carson what an expert he was on marriage. Jackie Mason, another guest, spoke up. "You're not an expert on marriage," he corrected him. "You're an expert on divorce."

I also like the crack made by the comedy writer Mel Brooks: Hollywood is really two Newarks.

On the other hand, the distinguished anthropologist Ashley Montagu always talks common sense in a highly entertaining manner. In a discussion about sex and its problems he agreed that alcohol could be a help inasmuch as it loosens inhibitions and reduces intellectual powers. Most astute was his next remark. "The *only* true aphrodisiac," he said, "is variety."

Jonathan Winters is an original comedian, but he has to have the right setup to be funny. His best shows were with Jack Paar. Yet the Jonathan Winters style has influenced other performers; his mannerisms are often imitated, and not often acknowledged.

I got a kick out of Robert Morse when he came on the Carson show. He told about having little children who watch television commercials and always want what they hear discussed.

They came to their father with a new request.

"We want bad breath," they said.

And on another show, comic Joe E. Lewis remarked that Barbra Streisand was his choice to play the life of Jimmy Durante.

It is a cheerful sight for me to see John Bubbles, the Negro song and dance man, on television. Like ole man river, he keeps on rolling along.

As far back as 1922 I saw him in vaudeville, when he was half of a team known as Buck and Bubbles. His improvised dancing was always a wonder, and I am glad to note that his singing voice has not been impaired by age.

Bubbles created the original role of Sportin' Life in the 1935 Gershwin opera *Porgy and Bess,* and it has never been equaled by anyone since.

The rehearsals for that historic opera created one incident that bears repeating. With his untrained talent, Bubbles could not read music; consequently, he had to be taught his role note by note.

Alexander Smallens, the conductor, became exasperated at one point and threw up his hands in despair. Wishing to placate him, Bubbles made an attempt at a compliment: "Mr. Smallens," he said, "if I had the money of the way you conduct, I'd be a millionaire."

From time to time I watch the former middle-weight champion Rocky Graziano on TV. He is one of my favorites, always entertaining and likable.

The story of his life is well-known to fight fans and moviegoers—Paul Newman gave a memorable portrayal as Graziano in *Somebody Up There Likes Me*. A tough kid from Brooklyn, Graziano had fought his way up and into the fight ring and in and out of the army and jail.

When he lost the title to Sugar Ray Robinson, Graziano decided to hang onto his money and retire. In the early television days he worked as a comic with Martha Raye, and he still shows up on the Merv Griffin show.

He told Merv that he works to help juvenile delinquents (he had a hell of a time pronouncing the word "delinquent").

"What advice do you give them?" asked Merv.

"I tell 'em to have a good alibi and get a good lawyer," quipped Graziano.

Peter Ustinov is a great favorite of mine. There is nothing he cannot do superlatively—act, write, direct, perform. His unerring ear for music and languages makes him an amusing raconteur.

I first met Peter in Hollywood during the time of the televised Senator McCarthy hearings. His imitations of McCarthy and Attorney Joseph Welch were great party entertainment.

In the many years that I have been committed to various mental hospitals I have changed greatly. Not long ago I met Peter Ustinov, after a lapse of eight years. "Why," he exclaimed in well-simulated pleasure, "it's Oscar Levant!"

"Formerly Oscar Levant," I said.

Certain people act on me like an emetic. Phyllis Diller, the so-called comedienne, for example. I treasure every moment that I do not see her.

On the short side, there is my crack about Jack E. Leonard, the corpulent comedian. "Jackie lives by bread alone."

I admire Sammy Davis, Jr., and his wide-ranging talents, but sometimes I think he goes out of his way to please. When he had Elizabeth Taylor and Richard Burton on his TV show, it proved to be a dismal event—even though Richard Burton can charm the pants off everyone. Including Elizabeth Taylor.

I am also convinced that Perry Como's voice comes out of his eyelids.

However, in this uncertain world of ours, we can always be sure of one thing. Flipping the dial of a television set on a Sunday evening between eight and nine, there will always be the statue that talks like a man. Ed Sullivan will last as long as other people have talent.

I used to believe I was the first one to do political satire on the radio—but I have been undeceived. It was really Will Rogers. However, I can say that I was the first to do political satire on television. Rogers and TV did not coincide.

My best appearances on radio were with Fred Allen's show. But everyone can say that. Fred was such a superb performer and his scripts were so good. I must add that at supper after his first show of one season he was the most disconsolate man I have ever seen.

"I've used up all my material for that first show," he moaned. "I've got nothing left. What can I do for the next show?" He went on, nevertheless, to do quite well for a long period of years.

When I appeared on the radio show *Information Please,* Arnold Schoenberg, with whom I had studied a year before in California, wrote me a letter in April, 1939, saying in part:

> I was told you became a great man in New York. I listened to you several times on the radio but could not recognize your voice. I also heard that you conducted very successfully. [A reference to a movie short I conducted for the World's Fair, directed by Joseph Losey.] Now, was it not a good idea of mine when I forced you to do it with the Federal? Many greetings.

The reference to the Federal was a concert that I had given in Los Angeles for the W.P.A., conducting a symphonic piece that I had composed under Schoenberg's guidance.

By October of the same year I received another letter from Mr. Schoenberg in which he wrote: "How are you? Do you compose? Do you still remember that you studied with me? I hear you sometimes on 'Information Please' which amuses me very much."

Naturally I was delighted to hear from the great man. I was also gratified that he finally recognized my voice.

Appearing on *Information Please* did more than propel me into my first role as a "talk" panelist. It provided me with the opportunity for meeting the outstanding men and women who appeared on the show.

One such person was the author Christopher Morley, the essayist whose best-selling novel, *Kitty Foyle,* also served as the movie vehicle for an Academy Award win by Ginger Rogers. Morley, one of three brothers from Pennsylvania, all Rhodes scholars, was also a contributing editor for the *Saturday Review.*

After Morley appeared on one show he wrote me a letter asking me to compose a sinfonietta "representing the charms, indignations, despairs, and general mystery of the White Collar Girl"—the type of girl that *Kitty Foyle* represented.

Unfortunately, I was too busy with concerts and additional work on my own piano concerto to take on more chores.

Another person I met during the days of *Information Please* was Irwin Edman, the late philosophico-literary professor of Columbia University, who was destined for his career from the beginning. His sister once told me that their parents realized when Edman was a little boy that he was different from everybody else. Unlike modern-day psychology-oriented parents, they refused to fret because their son did not fall into an accepted pattern. Instead, he was allowed to pursue his natural interests and consequently was brought up just right to be a philosopher. I liked Professor Edman also for the reason that he sent me one of his books inscribed: "To the liveliest of the philosophers."

Anyone who appears on TV—or, in the old days, on radio—becomes fair game for the critics. Often they suffer doom from sheer inadvertence. Jan Struther, the English novelist, was a favorite of ours on *Information Please* during its radio heyday when it won every award going. Her visits stopped abruptly after a particular broadcast. She mentioned a good book by Agatha Christie, actually a superb mystery. Hundreds of letters came in to protest her appearance—yet the poor woman was entirely innocent. The book she talked about was *Ten Little Indians*. Jan had unconsciously used the title of the English edition which was *Ten Little Niggers*. Incidentally, it was moderator Clifton Fadiman who protested the caricature of a Jewish matron on Fred Allen's old show. This supersensitivity of the Jews about their race has now been inherited by the Negroes.

I used to take walks with the famous Dr. Karl Menninger. I recall his concern over the fact that his daughter had married a Jewish doctor. I comforted him. It reminded me of the time when Max Beerbohm was asked if he were Jewish. He rose nobly to the occasion. "I regret to say," he said, "that I have not a drop of Jewish blood in my body."

Actually, being part Jewish is rather popular these days. Robert Lowell, in whose veins flows most of the bluest blood in New England, confided to me that he had a few drops of Jewish blood—which makes him the all-American poet.

Very few people knew that Douglas Fairbanks, Sr. (Douglas Ullman), was half-Jewish—which makes Douglas Fairbanks, Jr., the toast of the British Empire, at least a quarter Jewish.

I understand that Richard Burton and Elizabeth Taylor have great arguments over who is more Jewish. Burton claims that he is; his grandfather was half Jewish. Elizabeth insists that she has the edge—she embraced the Jewish faith when she was married to Mike Todd.

Buddy Hackett, the comedian who is *really* Jewish, said with a blast, "The reformed Jews only recognize *five* of the Ten Commandments!"

In that Las Vegas fracas where Frank Sinatra came off second best with a fellow named Cohen, the comic Henny Youngman quipped, "Sinatra should never fight a Jew in the desert!"

Henny also mentioned that the Israeli war was so short-lived that Bob Hope didn't have a chance to entertain the troops.

On the other hand, the drama coach Stella Adler went too far with her absurd remark to aspiring actresses: "If you are not Jewish or Italian you might just as well forget it."

And Groucho Marx makes no secret of his opinion of Jewish performers who use their race to get cheap laughs. He thinks they are more offensive than funny.

But there is certainly no doubt about the fact that Yiddishism has penetrated the English language.

The use or abuse of language in humor has always fascinated me. My favorite word in English is *désolé*. I remember that the first time the word "schmo" was used on the Fred Allen radio show it shocked the proper Jewish families immeasurably. It is a Yiddish contraction of an unprintable word. And "nuts," so common an expletive now that it is almost obsolete, was considered so dirty in my youth that I was forbidden to use it.

My concern for words was shared by the father of George Gershwin, quite a wit in his own right, who once interrupted a conversation by saying nostalgically: "By the way, whatever happened to 'Oh, fudge!' " There was also the notorious time when Woollcott used the word "pubescent" on his radio program and got a clutch of complaining letters from listeners who thought it was obscene. I marvel to think of how sophisticated the average American audience has become since then.

I have no idea where Gershwin's "Oh, fudge!" went, but I can tell where it came from. Disraeli says that an old pamphlet entitled *Remarks upon the Navy* declares:

There was in our time (Charles II) one Captain Fudge, commander of a merchantman (Black Eagle), who upon his return from a voyage, how ill fraught soever his ship was, always brought home his owners a good crop of lies; so much that now, aboard ship, the sailors when they hear a great lie told, cry out, "You fudge it."

I knew Ben Hecht, the writing child of the century, rather well. I was of two minds about him, one of them favorable. Hecht used to play the violin very badly. He used to think it funny to have an orchestra come up to his home at Nyack, New York, and have his friends watch him saw away with them. To me it was sheer torture.

Everything was a gag with Ben Hecht. He and his friends, which included his writing collaborator Charlie MacArthur, were an "in" group of the time.

I met Hecht first in the twenties when he was trying to reform an eccentric dancer. That is, he was trying to make an intellectual out of him. It was an effort that was doomed from the beginning.

In the thirties, Hecht and MacArthur wrote and produced several movies at the Long Island studios of Paramount Pictures.

I wrote some of the background music for one of the pictures, *Crime Without Passion,* that had Claude Rains and Margo in the cast. For this endeavor, I received a token salary of fifteen dollars a week along with the overblown title of Assistant President of the Music Department. Also, part of my job was to play duets once a week with Ben.

I went along with the gag for a while, then I finally asked for a raise. Hecht sent me a memo that my salary was to be doubled. My paycheck remained the same. Every time I complained, I got a memo announcing a big increase in wages, yet the real money never changed. It was all great fun, but I finally quit.

"I can't afford such a high salary," I told him. "I'm starving to death as it is!"

In the forties, when June and I were first married, we lived in a very nice hotel. Hecht called and asked if he could use our apartment to try out readings for a new picture.

I said okay. Ben came up, followed by Henry Hull, who was a prominent actor then and still is a pleasure to watch. Hecht gave him the script (for which, incidentally, he wanted me to write the music). He asked Hull to try a few lines. Hull scowled. "You know my work, don't you?" he demanded. "I don't read for anybody." And he left, almost slamming my door.

What I want to know and never have been able to find out is why Hecht wanted to use *my* apartment as a reading room. Whatever the reason was, the picture was called off and much later was made at Columbia Studios with Douglas Fairbanks, Jr.

Ben Hecht and I had not met nor seen each other for many years. In 1958 when I began my Los Angeles television show, he must have been in California, for he wrote a lengthy piece about me for *Esquire* magazine. A few samples follow:

The world was obviously going to pot with an Easter bunny in its hand, a glad-glad burbling everywhere. And nothing could be done about it.

Then along came Oscar Levant—the Bad-Taste Kid. Instead of simper, snarl. Instead of back scratching, rump-kicking. Instead of panting obeisance to the bobbery codes of television, ill-mannered snorts. A more revolutionary figure has not been seen since Guy Fawkes.

. . . all the other cautious self-advertisers seem much more boastful than our vainglorious Oscar. The reason is obvious. These other performers actually admire themselves. Oscar, though he boasts an hour and a half without stopping, does not admire himself. On the contrary, he is full of contempt for himself. And, good neurotic that he is, he is willing to share this contempt with the world.

Thus Oscar, with all his neuroses going like a stage full of juggler's platters, manages to emerge cannily as a fellow of golden heart and no meanness.

In 1958 Los Angeles had a paper (now defunct), the *Mirror News*. An ad in the personal column carried this notice: "Attractive divorcé is looking for a husband, must like Oscar Levant, drives in the country, and music." My comment was: "I'd like to meet a man like that myself."

In that year I was at NBC doing the Eddie Fisher show (that's when shows were live). I got a call from Jerry Lewis asking if he could appear on my local show that same evening. Of course I agreed. Jerry came on the show and was never funnier.

On my desk I had a book of poems by T. S. Eliot with a picture of the author on the dust cover. Jerry took one look at the picture—put on glasses, pursed his lips, then proceeded to read the poetry in a crazy imitation of how he thought Eliot would sound. Very hysterical.

We then paused, as they say, for a commercial. It was a car commercial, one of those little French ones so popular then. As I did the lead-in Jerry gagged it up.

"Gary Cooper uses them for cuff links," he yelled.

So, for the remainder of the show, I referred to the car as Gary Cooper cuff links.

The next day the doorbell rang at my house and a beautiful young girl announced herself.

"I'm Maria Cooper," she said. "My father wants Mr. Levant to have this," and she handed June a letter and a small box.

The box contained a pair of gold cuff links initialed G.C., shaped, believe it or not, like little cars with diamonds for headlights. The letter read:

Dear Oscar:
   The family and I love your shows—you leave 'em with suspense. But natch, last night's was a topper.
   Thanks for the *plug* too.

Just thought you might get a kick out of having these links—will tell you about them sometime.

Best always,
Gary Cooper

Jerry Lewis also wrote me an ecstatic letter about his appearance on the show—how he respected me, was charmed by my wife, what fun, what an education it was, etc., etc. Further, he invited me to appear as a guest on his first show of the coming season.

On the strength of his invitation I canceled the Fisher shows that I was asked to do, and then inexplicably Jerry Lewis reneged on his promise.

Well, to quote an Englishman, sometimes I get so mad I could shake Switzerland!

At the peak of my television career I had, I must confess, wild acclaim. Three television critics who devoted a great deal of space to me in their columns were Hal Humphrey of the Los Angeles *Times,* Don Freeman of the San Diego *Times-Union,* and Jack O'Brian of the late New York *Journal American.*

When I returned to TV in 1960 my show was bought for syndication. I announced on the air: "This is Oscar Levant in Meet the Mess. This is Oscar Levant, who has made insanity America's favorite hobby. My show is now syndicated. It goes to the Menninger Clinic in Topeka, Bellevue in New York, and the psychiatric ward at Mt. Sinai in Los Angeles."

I then explained the difference between a psychoanalyst and a psychiatrist: "You tell your problems to a psychoanalyst and he says it isn't your fault. Tell the same problems to a psychiatrist and he says it is your fault."

Don Freeman wrote:

Oscar Levant is back on television. . . . Speaking not as a dispassionate reviewer but as a fan of long standing, I say this is perfectly wonderful news.

. . . Groucho Marx once dispatched a wire to Levant: "Listening to you is like opening a dusty room and allowing fresh air to blow in." And that it is. Welcome back, Oscar.

Another time I declared on TV, "The secret of my marriage to June is that neither of us can stand me."

"If I knew what your problems were, I'd make medical history," replied June.

I then proceeded to explain to her that killing people was a sex thrill—except in executions, which takes the sex out of it.

"You learn something every day," commented June.

Steve Allen came aboard to plug his book. As this was in 1960, June kiddingly suggested that Steve and I run for President and Vice-president. "Outside of the two candidates, I can't think of anyone more inadequate than us," I observed.

John Crosby, writing for the New York *Herald Tribune,* noted:

> Mr. Levant, who is the original sick comedian, can make me laugh. Of course, he can make me wince, too. It is the nature of laughter that it is composed, at least partly, of shock—little sparks of total irrelevance and electricity and wit and reminiscence, impossible to pin down in print.

And Ben Gross of the New York *Daily News* had this to say: "This brilliant, grumpy fellow is a joy to hear. His wife, June, is the television find of the season. More than a mere feeder of lines, she's charming, patient and completely understanding. . . . I like June."

Jack Dempsey came on my show, and I reminded the audience that in the second Dempsey-Tunney fight the referee's count was as long as the slow movement of Beethoven's Ninth Symphony.

Gore Vidal was another guest, "Let me ask you a 1940-type question," I inquired. "Have you ever been psychoanalyzed?"

"I'll give you a 1960 answer," Gore replied. "No."

Once on TV I had as a guest the octogenarian dancer Ruth

St. Denis, who had known the legendary dancer Isadora Duncan.

I said to Miss St. Denis, "Let's not repeat the hackneyed exchange between Isadora Duncan and G. B. Shaw." You know the one: Isadora Duncan, a firm believer in eugenics, said to Shaw, "With your brains and my looks we could have the perfect child." To which Shaw replied, "It could have your brains and my looks."

At any rate, Miss St. Denis and I agreed not to tell the story, but Pamela Mason, the other guest on the show, stammered through it anyway.

The litigious Pamela has a reputation for being amusing and articulate. During one of my more jubilant periods, she remarked, "If I had nineteen lovers, you would *not* be one of them!"

When I invited Laurence Stallings to appear on television with me, it was the occasion of our first and only meeting. In the course of the broadcasted conversation, I mentioned that I preferred Turgenev to Tolstoi.

"You are," he said, "an inverted snob"—and of course he was right.

Also appearing with me on those shows were politicians, on the national as well as the local level. A short but amusing note came in from the actress Audrey Totter.

"Dear Oscar," she wrote, "If you keep endorsing Judge Ross 'fulsomely,' he'll probably take away your narcotic license." It made me laugh (which doesn't happen very often).

Hermione Gingold, the well-preserved actress, is unique with her fey humor. I had her appear with me on TV a few times. As she smoked a cigar, we discussed our most intimate problems openly. She was the one who originated the remark about Elsa Maxwell: "Just another pretty face."

She came bustling on scene once and told me she had just been to her dentist and that her gums were still bleeding. "You still have blood?" I said in admiration. Hermione started her career in English cabarets and always revels in close contact. It was Noel Coward who sent her a telegram for one opening. It read: I AM OUT FRONT. TREMBLE.

By 1961 my health had deserted me again, and I discontinued all performing.

In May of that year Jack O'Brian in the New York *Journal American* began a campaign.

BRING BACK OSCAR LEVANT was emblazoned at two different times over his column. From the first:

> Our wonderment if many people share our suspicion that Oscar Levant is sorely missed on N.Y. TV has been answered most emphatically: We've received more mail full of "Bring Back Oscar Levant" appeals than any in years—he does radiate a raffish integrity. . . . He has true wit, and a beautiful wife who takes none of his incisive guff. . . . Oscar's our favorite prodigal, a black sheep we need back in the N.Y. TV fold.

From the second O'Brian column:

> He has given TV some of its brightest moments—He makes a consistent point of seeming hopelessly irascible but he even has heroes, pleasantly unexpected ones. He has the capacity to enthuse as much as his famous faculty for criticism, which ranges from bludgeon to rapier. He presents an unusual and welcome point of view for TV—the man of angry honesty—but he is more than that—here are a few of the opinions of folks who have stuck in their three and four cents-worth on the subject of Oscar Levant. . . .

The name of Nat Hentoff, the writer, at the top of a list of more than twenty-five people concluded O'Brian's long column.

Praise from O'Brian is flattery indeed. To say that I was deeply touched would only be an understatement.

By 1963 I was well enough to go to New York at Jack Paar's

invitation to appear on his weekly show. Among the comments was this from Hal Humphrey in the Los Angeles *Times:* ". . . for the record let's add that a sick Oscar Levant made for more stimulating TV viewing than has been seen on the so-called entertainment shows this season."

There were three more trips to New York for Jack Paar, with the reruns totaling seven appearances in all.

In spite of a clash over material now and then, Paar was an extremely generous host with a unique ability for generating audience enthusiasm.

Paar wrote in his book *Three on a Toothbrush:*

> Oscar likes to appear on television. As Groucho Marx said of him, an ounce of attention is worth a pound of cure. Sick or well, Levant likes to talk. And, oddly enough, he likes to be paid for it.
> S. N. Behrman has mentioned the "spiked embrace" of Levant's friendship, and I have a few scars to show for it myself. I remarked to Oscar that a humorist is just a comic who scratches. "No," he said, "a humorist is someone like you who has four writers and then ad-libs."

During those years Jack Paar was the only person to give me a professional tumble. He pulled me out of the darkness of the sickroom; but when I ceased being a helpless invalid, he switched to Bobby Kennedy. Paar likes tragic figures.

One of the phrases of which I am fondest is The Unloved One. But not as applied to myself. (I'm a one-man love-in.) All the same, it seems that I am determined, by hook or crook, to be unloved. Harry Golden, the Jewish Southerner who edits his writings in the Carolinas, visited the late Carl Sandburg. He told him he was coming North and would visit me. "Do you want me to give Oscar a message?" he asked.

"Yes," Sandburg said, "give him a hug."

So Golden arrived, and damned if he did not give me a hug just before he left. It was the first hug I had had for many years.

Everyone wants to get me outside the house. The reason they

always give is that I "must get out into the fresh air." I resisted this for a long while, for nearly five years, and then just to satisfy them, I went outside. I discovered the fact that there is no longer any such thing as fresh air.

But of late I have not only calmed down; I have been afflicted with a kind of creeping mellowness. Even my wife says so. Which reminds me of when I recently saw a married lady friend of mine. "Give Freddy my love," I said. "And you know what *that's* worth," I added.

So, as for me—

Oh, man,
Give me Chopin.

INDEX

Index

Index

Index